IMAGES
of America

MADISON COUNTY

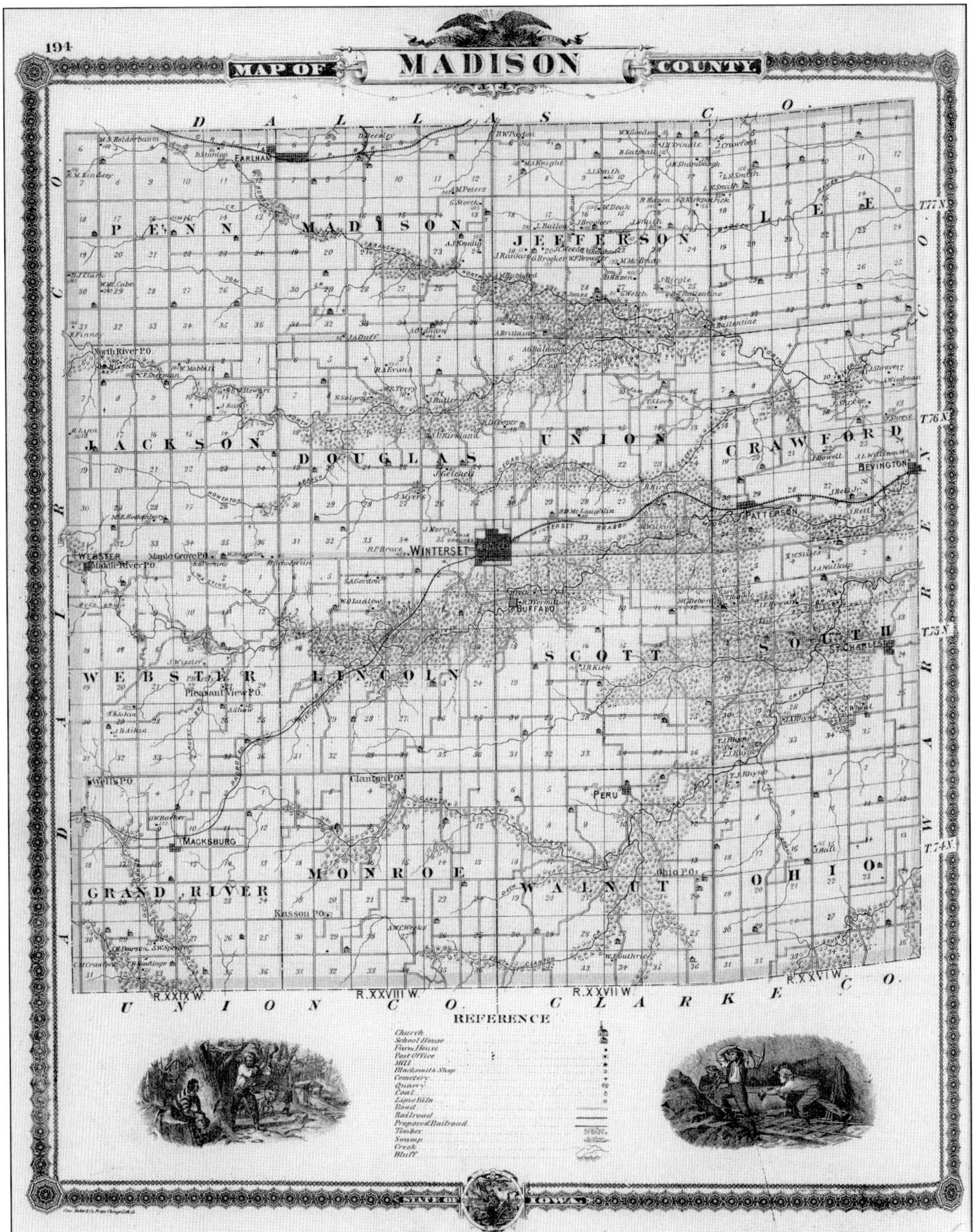

Madison County at a Glance. Madison County in south-central Iowa is laid out in an orderly grid system and is comprised of 16 townships. This township map dates to 1875. (Courtesy Madison County Historical Society.)

On the Cover: Covered Bridge to Steel Bridge. Around 1906, crews working northwest of Winterset replaced the Rose-Dunmire covered bridge with a steel one. The bridges on Creamery Road spanned the North River six miles southeast of Earlham. After its steel replacement was put into service, the Rose-Dunmire covered bridge was sold for salvage. (Courtesy Madison County Historical Society.)

IMAGES
of America

MADISON COUNTY

Darcy Dougherty Maulsby

ARCADIA
PUBLISHING

ISBN 978-1-4671-0622-1

Published by Arcadia Publishing
Charleston, South Carolina

Printed in the United States of America

Library of Congress Control Number: 2020946884

For all general information, please contact Arcadia Publishing:
Telephone 843-853-2070
Fax 843-853-0044
E-mail sales@arcadiapublishing.com
For customer service and orders:
Toll-Free 1-888-313-2665

Visit us on the Internet at www.arcadiapublishing.com

This book is dedicated to the pioneers, farmers, entrepreneurs, historians, visionaries, and assorted characters who have shaped Madison County and created this remarkable place that continues to thrive today.

Contents

ACKNOWLEDGMENTS

Great things in history are rarely done by any one person. They are accomplished by a team.

Many of the wonderful images in this book came from two extensive photograph collections, including the personal collection of Gary and Shirley Allen of Winterset and the archives of the Madison County Historical Society in Winterset.

I am also grateful to everyone who contributed photographs representing their communities, including Maxine Bussanmas from Bevington, Steve Downs from St. Charles, Jackie Leckband and the Earlham Historical Society, and Ralph and Georgena Breakenridge from Macksburg.

Then there are the photographers who helped round out images for the book: Todd Scott ("Drone Guy"), Jean Sherrard-Fifo of Covered Bridges Winery, Teddy Yaeger of Teddy Yaeger Photography, Stacy Zacharias of Stacy Z Photography, Wayne Davis, and Beth Gray.

I was blessed to work with many dedicated community leaders and wonderful organizations, including the *Winterset Madisonian* (Vicki Minor, managing editor), Madison County Parks (Amy Warnke, naturalist/education coordinator), the Iowa Quilt Museum (Megan Barrett, director), the Madison County Chamber of Commerce (Heather Riley, executive director), John Wayne Birthplace Museum (Brian Downes, executive director), The Iowa movie theater (Marianne Fons), St. Patrick's Irish Settlement Catholic Church (Dan Hanrahan), St. Charles Welcome Center (Joan Brown), and Pammel Park Coffee (Matt Hupton).

I also relied on many local historians, including Jared McDonald, director of the Madison County Historical Society; David Hargrove, director of the Winterset Public Library; and Linda Griffith Smith and Roslea Johnson of the Madison County Historic Preservation Commission. I would like to offer a big shout-out to the Madison County Historical Society staff, including Debbie Zacharias for scanning many of the images in this book.

It has been so much fun taking this deep dive into Madison County history. I am forever grateful to Madison County natives Jared McDonald and Linda Griffith Smith for their willingness to arrange meetings, tours, and informal "lunch and learns" each time I have traveled to Madison County.

While I have done my best to record Madison County history accurately, the research continues. Thanks to the Arcadia Publishing team, including my title manager Caroline Anderson, for helping preserving this tremendous legacy for generations to come.

Introduction

Say the name "Madison County," and many people think of covered bridges, a book, or a movie. All that is definitely part of Madison County, and yet this remarkable place is so much more. This is truly a slice of Americana, where you can step back in time and yet be very much in the present. It is a bit magical, actually.

Part of Madison County's magic is due to its geography. Located in south-central Iowa, the region is rustic and rural, yet its close proximity to Interstates 35 and 80 means Madison County is just minutes from the vibrant Des Moines metro area.

The stunning terrain of Madison County includes a unique mix of farm fields, gently rolling hills that are ideal for cattle grazing, and an abundance of timber, rivers, and creeks, some of which still include the iconic covered bridges that have graced these areas since the 1870s and 1880s.

Madison County is also richly endowed with a variety of rock resources, including limestone, that are suitable for building construction. This is reflected in the early architectural heritage of the county, which has been described as a legacy in stone.

Madison County was formed in 1846, the same year Iowa achieved statehood. It was named in honor of James Madison, the fourth president of the United States, who is known as the father of the US Constitution.

The first settler in Madison County, Hiram Hurst, offers an intriguing story, depending on who is telling it. This pioneer from Buchanan County, Missouri, staked a claim in what is now Crawford Township on the eastern side of the county on April 1, 1846. He built a little shack in the timber and cultivated a small patch of corn that spring and summer, according to a retrospective on the front page of the 1949 centennial edition of the *Winterset Madisonian* newspaper.

In the fall of 1846, he returned to his old home in Missouri. "It has been reported that he was a fugitive from justice, when he came to this county," the paper noted. His contemporaries told a different story, though, including Samuel Fife, a highly respected Civil War soldier and Madison County settler:

"Some of the early settlers tried to make out that Hurst was a criminal, that he had stolen hogs in Missouri," Fife states in Herman A. Mueller's 1915 book *History of Madison County, Iowa and its People*. "Others said he had burned a building and had to leave Missouri. My understanding was that he got into an altercation with a man in Missouri and nearly killed him. While here he was a very quiet man, had good judgment and was of a fine family. His family here was composed of a wife and four little boys. I have worked for him several times and have always found him a gentleman and his wife a perfect lady."

While Hurst did not stay in Madison County, choosing instead to move to Nebraska, eventually other settlers made Madison County their home. They took pride in their work as they built respectable farms, towns, churches, schools, businesses, civic organizations, and more.

One of those pioneers, Joseph H. Mack, arrived in 1856 in southwest Madison County and operated a sawmill until 1861. He then moved to Cincinnati, Ohio, where he studied medicine before returning to Madison County as a physician. Dr. Mack's influence on the physical health and moral character of the community was tremendous, from his efforts to promote education to his support for churches.

In 1875, while Dr. Mack was out of the region, a man named Mr. Greenwood had started a saloon in Macksburg. Dr. Mack's displeasure with such an intrusion into the community was quickly apparent the day of his return. By nightfall, he had a petition signed by most of the townspeople to stop the saloon. The next morning, Mack presented the petition to Greenwood, along with an offer to purchase the saloon for $55, the amount Greenwood had invested (roughly $1,300 in 2020).

Promising he would run a decent place, Greenwood politely refused the offer. In the interest of civility, Mack advised Greenwood that the town's ladies were implacably against permitting the saloon to operate. Mack cautioned Greenwood that he would soon face the town's most imposing force.

After a prayer meeting at the Baptist church, 18 of Macksburg's women filed into the saloon at its opening to discuss the issue with Greenwood. The type of persuasion used by the group is unrecorded. Within minutes of their arrival, however, Greenwood searched out Mack and immediately sold the property to him for $55. Mack turned the saloon over to the women, who piled all the furnishings and the saloon sign in the street. They celebrated the demise of the town's first saloon with a bonfire.

This story reflects the community spirit, grit, and cooperation that have endured in Madison County for generations. It remains a place where friends and neighbors work together for the common good. Just ask Heather Riley, executive director of the Madison County Chamber of Commerce:

"I love that this community has so many stories to tell," said Riley, whose family moved to Winterset in 2005. "There's the story of a novel and Hollywood movie putting a rural Iowa community on the map, the story of Susan B. Anthony advocating for women's voting rights from our courthouse steps, and the story about a Winterset High School graduate who made his mark on the world with a crew of 'Monuments Men' who saved priceless works of art from being looted and destroyed by the Nazis during World War II. I also love that our community is full of big thinkers who dream big and put in the work to make things happen."

While Madison County is famous for its covered bridges, there are plenty of other don't-miss attractions. "Without a doubt our county and city parks are absolutely hidden gems," Riley noted. "A trip to Madison County is not complete without a visit to Pammel State Park and a few hours of exploration along Middle River. The Winterset City Park is a beautiful, wide-open space featuring lots of picnic areas, mature trees, walking paths, an English hedge maze and places to spread out and enjoy nature."

All this contributes to the incredible quality of life that is enhanced by the abundance of fun things to do. On any given weekend, there are concerts, farmers markets, pancake breakfasts, scavenger hunts, wine tastings, fundraising events, auctions, and more.

All this creates the charm of Madison County. Come along on a journey to explore the county's past, present, and future and experience the magic for yourself.

One

Building on a Solid Foundation
The Quarry Story

While few things in life are set in stone, that is not the case in Madison County. This is limestone country, thanks to an ancient sea that once covered this region.

As the plants and tiny sea creatures lived and died, their remains helped form the rock that was deposited in this area during the Pennsylvanian geological period, roughly 300 million years ago. Since the last glacier that pushed into Iowa thousands of years ago stopped just north of modern-day Interstate 80, the limestone in Madison County was not buried by glacial sediments.

In the Earlham area, exposed limestone seams could be found at the surface. In other areas, the limestone was in ravines where a creek or river had eroded the land.

Stone quarrying became an essential industry in Madison County starting in the mid-1800s, as settlers relied on local materials to build homes, barns, schools, and more. The construction of Madison County's first stone courthouse in the late 1860s led to an influx of stonemasons. There was plenty of work for skilled masons like Caleb Clark, one of Madison County's settlers, and David Harris, who also owned a quarry.

When the state capitol in Des Moines was being built between 1871 and 1886, stone was shipped to Des Moines from Earlham, which was on the main line of the Chicago, Rock Island & Pacific Railroad.

Even though the stone building tradition in Madison County faded by 1885, quarrying remained prevalent. By 1896, the industry thrived around Earlham, Winterset, and Peru before the advent of cement block and poured concrete construction.

A number of independent quarries operated in Madison County into the early 20th century, although the Great Depression and World War II ended most of them. The remains of old mining equipment are still visible, however, around the Peru area.

Today, only Martin Marietta Inc. continues to mine limestone in Madison County, with quarries near Winterset and Earlham. The company supplies various aggregates, including road stone. Still, much of Madison County's heritage remains a legacy in stone.

MINERS ON PERU QUARRY WALL. The mining industry began in the Peru area in the late 1800s. Limestone quarries provided a livelihood for many men. Picks, sledgehammers, shovels, mules, and sheer muscle were the tools of the trade in the early 1900s. At that time, the East Peru quarry contained an estimated two million cubic yards of rock. (Courtesy Madison County Historical Society.)

STONE CRUSHER AT PERU QUARRY. Once the limestone was extracted from the earth, it was run through a rock crusher. A spur rail line was built in 1903 from the main railroad tracks in East Peru to the quarry. In 1904, Des Moines received $8,000 worth of crushed stone from the Peru quarry to pave Grand Avenue. (Courtesy Madison County Historical Society.)

Limestone Courthouse on the Square. Madison County's log courthouse, built in 1849, was replaced by a stone courthouse constructed in 1868–1869. After a fire destroyed the building in 1875, a second, identical structure made of native limestone was constructed in 1876. The interior woodwork and twin staircases are made from locally milled oak and walnut. This courthouse still graces the town square and is listed in the National Register of Historic Places. (Courtesy Allen family.)

Bevington Stone Barn. Dr. Charles D. Bevington built this stone barn on the south edge of Winterset in 1856. Draft horses raised by Dr. Bevington were housed in the barn by the 1880s. During the first seven months of 1889, thirty-five train carloads of 20 horses each were shipped from Madison County to eastern markets. It is likely some of Bevington's horses were included in these shipments, which totaled 700 horses at an average of $125 each. (Author's collection.)

Bevington Stone Privy. This fancy privy was built in 1856 just yards from the mansion constructed on the south edge of Winterset by Dr. Charles D. Bevington. The privy is a "three holer" made of local limestone and native walnut woodwork. It is also one of just a few privies in America listed in the National Register of Historic Places. (Author's collection.)

Stone-Arch Bridge. Architect Ray F. Weirick designed this bridge and oversaw its construction in Winterset City Park in 1919–1920. The native limestone bridge is still in use today by vehicles and hikers returning from Clark Tower. It is one of three stone bridges constructed in the public park, which was first opened in 1872. (Courtesy Allen family.)

HISTORY SET IN STONE. This limestone historical marker at the entrance to the Madison County Historical Society highlights the history of Madison County, including the Sac and Fox Indians, the first settlers in 1846, courthouses, mills, the covered bridges, and the Delicious apple developed by Jesse Hiatt. The marker was provided by Penn-Dixie Quarry and the Winterset Monument Company in 1980. (Author's collection.)

NORTH RIVER STONE SCHOOLHOUSE. Built in 1874 of native limestone, this school was in continuous use until it closed in 1945. It is now listed in the National Register of Historic Places and has been open to the public since 1973. Located northwest of Winterset, the one-room school is 1.7 miles from the Hogback covered bridge. It was built by stonemason David Harris. The quoining (stacked masonry blocks) on the corners is a trademark of Harris's distinctive style. (Courtesy Madison County Historical Society.)

Clark Tower in Winterset Honors Pioneers. Located in the Winterset City Park, Clark Tower was built in 1926 as a memorial to honor one of Madison County's pioneer families. Constructed of native limestone, the tower stands 25 feet high and offers a commanding view of the Middle River valley below. (Author's collection.)

Elegant Stone Home. Winterset is filled with beautiful buildings made of native limestone, including this home at 223 South Front Street (now South John Wayne Drive). It was constructed in 1854–1855 for J.W. Vawter, one of the first merchants in Winterset, and his wife, Elizabeth. Vawter experienced financial difficulties during the Panic of 1857, and the couple left the community before 1865. The home later became a desirable rental property for new-to-town teachers. It is now a private residence. (Author's collection.)

Two

Love of the Land
Farming Takes Root in Madison County

When Hiram Hurst from Missouri became the first pioneer settler in Madison County, he planted a field of corn in Crawford Township in early April 1846. From then on, agriculture was an essential industry in Madison County.

"Reports came to us that the country up here was a fine place with good soil, nice rolling prairies, plenty of stone, an abundance of fine flowing springs and plenty of good timber along the streams," wrote W.S. Wilkinson in the May 19, 1904, edition of the *Winterset Madisonian* newspaper. "Early in the spring of 1848, my father and brother, Thomas, came to Madison County to locate a claim, and built a cabin within a few steps of a spring just one and one-half miles north of the center of Scott Township."

In the 1850s, Irish immigrants began settling in Lee Township and Crawford Township. St. Patrick's Church, which these immigrants built in 1868, continues to be a focal point in the area and is known for the 1979 visit of Pope John Paul II.

Progressive Madison County residents formed a county agricultural society in 1856. They successfully experimented with various grains, fruits, vegetables, cattle, sheep, hogs, and poultry. Corn became king and helped Madison County's livestock industry thrive. One county farmer, Jesse Hiatt, made a valuable contribution to the apple industry with the development of his Delicious apple.

Grain mills and a woolen mill near Winterset served local farmers as Madison County transitioned from subsistence farming to commercial production. These momentous changes in the farm economy could not have been possible without the railroad, which arrived in northern Madison County in 1869 and connected farms with markets near and far.

As farms expanded, towns developed throughout Madison County, along with country schoolhouses and rural churches. While all the country schools closed by the mid-20th century, some of the rural churches and small towns endure. Agriculture itself remains a vital industry. The county has 977 farms and produces $243.6 million in total ag sales, according to the 2017 US Department of Agriculture Census of Agriculture. In addition, 20 percent of the county's residents are employed in ag-related jobs.

ARROWHEADS FOUND IN MADISON COUNTY. While the Sac and Fox once lived in the area that would become Madison County, they signed a treaty in 1843 ceding their Iowa land to the federal government. Pioneer farmers arrived in Madison County by the spring of 1846. Through the years, people have uncovered traces of Native American heritage on the landscape, like these arrowheads found in Madison County that are on display at the Madison County Historical Society. (Author's collection.)

SHEEP AND WOOL WERE BIG BUSINESS. Sheep production in Iowa soared in the 1860s, propelled by the outbreak of the Civil War in April 1861. Wool was in high demand from the US Army, both for military uniforms and blankets. This advertisement from the 1869 Madison County Business Directory promotes White, Munger & Co., proprietors of Madison Woolen Mills in Winterset. The company manufactured tweeds, flannel, yarns, blankets, and more. (Courtesy Madison County Historical Society.)

Distinguished Sheep Producers. A combination of available farmland, low labor requirements, affordable corn, and a good climate for livestock production made Iowa an ideal place to expand the sheep industry in the 19th century. There must have been a special occasion for these men to pose with their prized livestock for this photograph, which is included in a history of the Foster Brothers' farming operation near Earlham. (Courtesy Earlham Historical Society.)

Gillespie Barn Dates to 1874. The Gillespie Barn west of Winterset on Highway 92 has been on the Iowa Barn Foundation's All-State Barn Tour for years. The property has been in the family since 1870. Shown here are, from left to right, Dan Ryner, Steve Gillespie, and Gillespie's sister Lori Gillespie Ryner. The barn was built in 1874 by W.W. George. It is on Old Bluff Road, which ran to Council Bluffs. (Author's collection.)

Madison County Poor Farm, 1876–2001. Madison County officials purchased 304 acres of land in 1876 to provide refuge for those struggling to meet their own survival needs. Residents raised grain, hay, horses, cattle, hogs, poultry, fruits, and vegetables to become more self-sufficient. In 1956, some of the property was leased to the Horton Nursing Home. Residential care programs continued until October 2001. The county sold the land in 2002. (Author's collection.)

Iowa Barn Tour Features McBroom Barn. Ron and Virginia McBroom are shown in 2018 at their historic barn, which is five miles south of Interstate 80 on Highway 169. The post-and-beam barn with wooden-peg construction was designed by I.F. Carter of De Soto. "It would be the largest barn in this part of the county," noted an 1884 Madison County newspaper. The barn has been featured on the Iowa Barn Foundation's All-State Barn Tour. (Author's collection.)

WINTERSET GRAIN ELEVATOR. Myles Young Sr. began operating a grain elevator in Winterset in 1884. The elevator was at the east end of Green Street and operated with steam power. The elevator, which specialized in the grain and coal business, was fairly close to the railroad depot. (Courtesy Madison County Historical Society.)

M. YOUNG FEED AND GRAIN. After moving from Illinois and establishing a grain elevator in Winterset in 1884, Myles Young Sr. expanded his business to include livestock feed and seed. In 1917, M. Young & Co. moved to a new location at North First and Green Streets, near downtown Winterset. Young's son Myles Jr. joined the company, which expanded to include specialized feed rations for livestock. From left to right are Myles Young Jr., J.W. Krell, and T.L. Bedwell. (Courtesy Allen family.)

Birthplace of the Delicious Apple. Jesse Hiatt and his wife, Rebecca (Pearson) Hiatt, arrived in Madison County about 150 years ago with a wagon full of fruit trees. Around 1872, Jesse Hiatt (1826–1898) noticed a little sprout growing between his rows of apple trees. This apple, which Hiatt called the Hawkeye, became the famous Delicious apple after winning the 1894 International New Fruit Fair hosted by Stark Brothers' Nursery in Louisiana, Missouri. (Both, courtesy of Madison County Historical Society.)

Descendant of Original Delicious Apple Tree Lives On. While Jesse Hiatt's famous Delicious apple tree died in 1940, a descendent of that tree grows just north of Peru. A stone marker at the site tells the story of this noteworthy tree. In nearby East Peru (with a population of approximately 125), a wooden welcome sign featuring a red apple showcases this noteworthy piece of Madison County ag history. (Author's collection.)

"Uncle Henry" Wallace Gained Fame in Madison County. Henry Wallace (1836–1916) was an active Presbyterian minister who served his last pastorate at the Presbyterian church in East Peru. He also farmed in southwest Iowa and accepted occasional speaking engagements. After he gave a speech in Winterset on July 4, 1878, he began writing a weekly column in the local newspaper and later became editor of the *Winterset Madisonian*. His progressive views on agriculture led him to publish the popular farm newspaper *Wallaces Farmer*. (Courtesy Library of Congress.)

Lenocker Family Hosted Reunions. Godfrey Lenocker moved to Madison County in 1869 from Illinois and bought 320 acres of virgin prairie near Earlham for $2 per acre. For years, Lenocker kept a diary of daily life on the farm. Lenocker family members gathered on August 22, 1908, to host a reunion. (Courtesy Ted Lenocker.)

Earlham Produced Stanley Plows. Tom Stanley began producing hand-powered plows in 1915 in Earlham. John McLennan went on the road in 1918 and sold the plows across a wide area. The plow shown here (the second type produced by Stanley) was patented in 1920. The Stanley Garden Plow Works factory produced 2,000 plows in 1920. Plows were produced in Earlham until the 1930s and then on a limited basis during World War II. (Author's collection.)

Penn Center Church Endures. The faithful gathered long before the Penn Center United Methodist Church was built in 1919. Reverend Hestwood from Winterset preached in the Penn Center schoolhouse prior to 1869. In 1872, Rev. James Lisle became the first pastor at an annual salary of $104. At this time, Penn Center shared the preaching circuit with Dexter, Earlham, Guthrie Center, and Stuart. The Penn Center church still serves the area. (Courtesy Earlham Historical Society.)

Farm Bureau Flourishes for 100-Plus Years. After the Iowa Farm Bureau Federation organized in 1918, local groups like the Madison County Farm Bureau formed. The organization's focus on creating a vibrant future for farm families and their communities attracted hundreds of new members within just a few years. Their enthusiasm is reflected in this photograph of a Madison County Farm Bureau picnic in Winterset on June 17, 1922. (Courtesy Madison County Historical Society.)

Corn Growers Broke Yields. This photograph featured in a history of the Foster Brothers' farming operation near Earlham shows the productivity of Madison County farms. "Record-breaking corn yield in the 1948 Madison County official 10-Acre Yield Contest. 175.3 bushels per acre. No commercial fertilizer used," reads the caption. In recent years, the average corn yield per acre in Madison County has totaled 166 bushels, according to the 2017 Census of Agriculture. In 2019, the statewide yield averaged 198 bushels per acre. (Courtesy Earlham Historical Society.)

John Deere Day in Winterset. John Deere Day was an annual event each winter, often around mid-January, at Powers Implement, which Maurice Powers opened in August 1953 at 213 North First Avenue. (An implement business had been at this location for 52 years by then.) John Deere Day events included a free lunch at the dealership, along with opportunities to see what was new in farm equipment and win door prizes. (Courtesy Allen family.)

Learning Life Skills. The Penn Gwens 4-H Club met monthly in members' homes in Penn Township. Older girls ran the meeting, which included educational programs about cooking, sewing, and public speaking. Club members in October 1955 at Linda Lenocker's house included, from left to right, (first row) Joy Neal, Judy Neal, Shirley Schafer, Marilyn Mount, and Marilyn Lawson; (second row) Gretchen Godby, Doris Ralston, Ruby Ralston, Judy Moore, and Dorothy Benz; (third row) Betty Kobolt, Mary Godby, Marilyn Ross, Connie Piatt, and Janice Lorimor. (Courtesy Joy Neal Kidney.)

John Deere Dealer Expands. The Winterset branch of the AgriVision Equipment Group is on the east edge of Winterset on Highway 92. AgriVision Equipment Group formed on January 1, 2014, with the merger of A&M Green Power Group and Barker Implement. The merger completed the consolidation of four longtime, family-owned John Deere dealerships into one operating unit. (Author's collection.)

Madison County Auction Serves Southwest Iowa. Hogs, cattle, sheep, and goats are sold at the Madison County Auction in Winterset, where regular sales occur each Tuesday. The first sale barn (North Sale Barn) started in 1933 near the junction of Highway 169 and Highway 92. Francis Jackson ran that sale barn and built the current sale barn at 1204 West Summit Street in 1947. Auctioneer Ernest "Ernie" Stowell operated the sale barn from 1953 through the mid-1980s. (Author's collection.)

Farm Safety 4 Just Kids. After Marilyn Adams's 11-year-old son Keith suffocated in a gravity-flow grain wagon during corn harvest in October 1986, the deadly accident inspired the rural Earlham mother to create Farm Safety 4 Just Kids (FS4JK). By 2012, the organization had promoted farm safety to more than six million people through more than 120 FS4JK chapters in America and Canada. Since 2016, the Progressive Agriculture Foundation has carried on FS4JK's mission. (Author's collection.)

Groth's Gardens and Greenhouses Thrive. Fourth-generation farmer Marvin Groth (Winterset High School class of 1971) and his wife, Deb (shown here), established Groth's Gardens and Greenhouses on the Groth family's century farm in 1993. They raise 4,000 mums each year and supply a wide array of other plants, including colorful flowers for the hanging baskets that grace downtown Winterset each summer. (Author's collection.)

COFFEE SHOP TALK. "Solving the world's problems" and discussing everything from grain prices to politics are time-honored traditions at rural Iowa's coffee shops and cafés. Note the seed-corn caps and winter gear worn by, from left to right, Dwight Downs, Kenneth McDonald, and Rich Gray, St. Charles–area farmers who gathered at a local restaurant. An Iowa Theater poster is taped to the wall. (Courtesy Steve Downs.)

ST. CHARLES AREA FARMERS IN THE FIELD. Working together is a tradition among Iowa farmers. These farmers brought their Allis Chalmers tractor and International Harvester equipment to a cornfield to get the work done. (Courtesy Steve Downs.)

St. Patrick's Church at the Irish Settlement. History abounds at St. Patrick's Church, which is in the part of Lee Township known as the Irish Settlement. The Catholic parish was created in 1852, and a log structure housed the first church. St. Patrick's Church, southwest of Cumming, was built in 1868 and is listed in the National Register of Historic Places. The church maintains an active congregation as well as St. Patrick's Cemetery. (Author's collection.)

Pope Visited Madison County. When Truro-area farmer Joe Hays wrote Pope John Paul II a letter, he invited him to Madison County during the Pope's 1979 American pilgrimage. The Holy Father accepted the invitation and gave an address at St. Patrick's Church on October 4, 1979. He urged generosity toward others in sharing the bounty of the land and stewardship in caring for the land for future generations. (Courtesy St. Patrick's Catholic Church.)

Madison County Fair. Generations of families have enjoyed the fun of the Madison County Fair, which is held for five days each July in Winterset. While the fair was not held during World War II, it was revived in 1947. 4-H and FFA members exhibit their livestock, and people of all ages enjoy entertainment options from pet shows to grandstand events at the fairgrounds, which are on the southwest side of Winterset. (Author's collection.)

Winterset FFA Inspires Students. FFA is the premier youth organization that prepares students for careers in agriculture. High schools across Madison County have FFA chapters. An FFA chapter was first established at Winterset High School in the 1930s, but it faded away by the early 1980s. The chapter was reestablished in 2004 and had 67 members by 2020. Chapter members participate in a variety of ag contests, community service activities, fundraising events, leadership and career development opportunities, and FFA Week, which includes Drive Your Tractor to School Day. (Courtesy Winterset FFA chapter.)

Cattle Country. Dan Hanrahan's family settled in Madison County in the 1870s. Hanrahan, a past president of the Madison County Farm Bureau and Madison County Cattlemen's Association, focuses on animal well-being and environmental stewardship in his cow-calf operation. "I'm always thinking, 'What can I do to improve the land? What can I do to improve the herd for those who come after me?' " said Hanrahan, who works with his parents, Richard and Virginia, and is shown here with his cattle in Crawford Township in July 2020. (Author's collection.)

Picking Grapes at Covered Bridges Winery. Vine-to-wine defines Covered Bridges Winery, along Highway 169 north of Winterset. Owners Kevin and Jean Fifo and their longtime friends Kevin and Rose Boyle began planting their first grapevines in 2004. Many of their wines honor Madison County's covered bridges. Imes Bridges is a port-styled dessert wine with an Iowa twist. Cedar Bridge is a semisweet blend with peach and apricot overtones. (Courtesy Covered Bridges Winery.)

Three

Guiding Freedom Seekers
The Underground Railroad

During the tumultuous antebellum and Civil War eras, Madison County was in the thick of the Underground Railroad. From 1857 to 1862, Madison County included multiple trails where freedom seekers could pass as safely as possible to the next stop. Stories endure of citizens' courageous efforts to fight slavery by "practical abolition," person by person, family by family.

Most of the Underground Railroad activities in Madison County took place in rural areas. Farmers and their families put their lives in danger to assist the freedom seekers on their journey to eastern Iowa and beyond into Canada.

Yet living among them were members of the Knights of the Golden Circle, a semi-military secret society that was active in Winterset, supporting the Confederacy and southern rights. This mix of wildly divergent political perspectives led to confrontations and near chaos in some instances.

Freedom seeker John Ross Miller's own account of a dramatic episode in Madison County was recorded in the summer 1934 *Annals of Iowa* (Vol. 19, No. 5) in the article "John Ross Miller" by C.C. Stiles:

> We had gone about two or three miles and was in a long lane when a crowd of men on horseback come on the run down the lane after us. They had shotguns and rifles and was raising an awful dust and making a lot of noise. We was shore some scared.
>
> They surrounded us and took us back to town, but they couldn't find any officers to put us in jail and while they were lookin' for the officers, they formed a ring around us boys to keep the crowd back. They got to talking pretty loud and someone dared any one to try to come inside that ring, and they hadn't more than said it than the coats began to fly and there wasn't any ring at all. The men that took us out of the ring gave us something to eat and told us which way to go, and we wasn't long in getting out of there.

At least one freedom seeker who had passed through Madison County returned after the Civil War ended. Charlie Moore, born into slavery in 1838, spent the last 50 years of his life as a resident and business owner in Winterset.

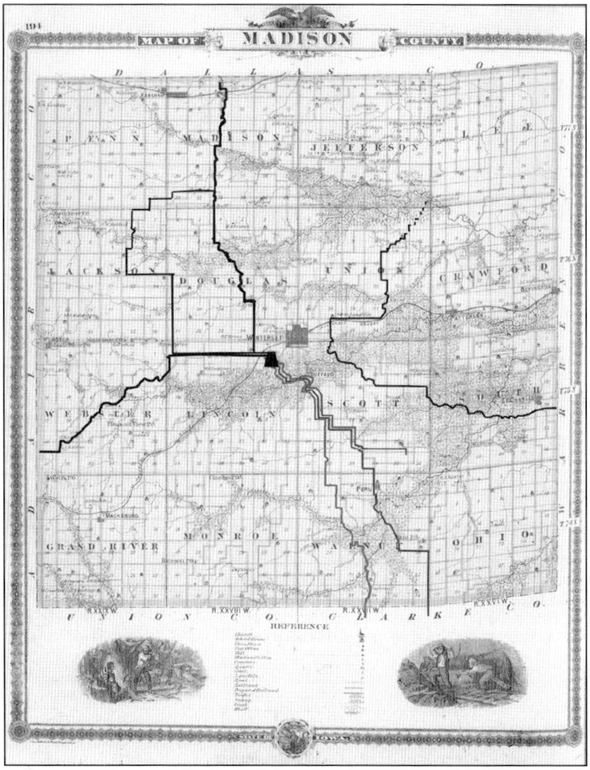

Routes through Madison County. Freedom seekers, also known as fugitive slaves or runaway slaves, who crossed Madison County were usually only here overnight before moving on to their next stop in Dallas or Warren Counties. Documented Underground Railroad stations have been found in 14 of Madison County's 16 townships. This map outlines some of the routes that freedom seekers took through Madison County. (Courtesy Madison County Historic Preservation Commission.)

Benjamin Franklin Roberts Home. This farmhouse was the hub of the Underground Railroad in Madison County. B.F. Roberts's farm was 1.5 miles west of Winterset, east of the four-way stop where Highways 169 and 92 diverge today. A room about 10 feet square was dug out on the north side of the basement kitchen. Fugitives sheltered behind a hidden door. The deteriorating stone house was demolished in 1939. (Courtesy Wayne Breeding.)

Rev. John Graham, Abolitionist. Scottish-born John Graham was a teacher, Presbyterian minister, and farmer who settled near Winterset with his wife, Mary (Small) Graham, in 1856. Graham was active in the Underground Railroad during the Civil War. Three of his sons and a son-in-law enlisted in the war. (All returned home safely.) Graham rejoiced in the emancipation of the slaves. He died in 1870 and is buried in the Winterset Cemetery. (Courtesy Madison County Historical Society.)

The Daring James Farris. James Farris, who settled in Union Township in 1851 with his wife, Elizabeth (Morgan) Farris, was one of the boldest of Madison County's Underground Railroad conductors. "He feared nothing," noted a 1915 history of Madison County. "He used to brag about his work and even publicly defied searching parties." In 2020, Rick Breeding of Winterset (left) and Kory Darnall of Davenport rededicate the gravestone of their ancestor, who died in 1870 and is buried in the Farris Cemetery in Union Township. (Courtesy Teddi Yaeger.)

Hogan Queen Home Still Stands. The Hogan Queen home west of St. Charles is a regal example of the limestone homes that often harbored runaway slaves in Madison County. Built at Queen's Point, the home was constructed around 1856 by Hogan and Martha (Runkle) Queen. It also served as a stagecoach stop. Stone for the building was quarried on the farm. The home's walnut staircase was made from trees harvested on the farm. (Courtesy Linda Griffith Smith.)

Charlie Moore Followed the North Star. Charlie Moore first passed through Madison County as a freedom seeker around 1860. After the Civil War he returned to Winterset, where he spent the last 50 years of his life working in the livery business, training horses, and selling Moore's Red Liniment, which promised to be "good for man or beast." When he died in 1920, Moore was buried in the Winterset Cemetery. In 2016, the Madison County Historic Preservation Commission installed this gravestone to honor Moore's legacy. (Author's collection.)

Four

Covered Bridges

Worldwide Fame

Not only is Madison County the "Covered Bridge Capital of Iowa," but its iconic wooden bridges have propelled Madison County to worldwide fame.

The story of the bridges dates back to 1870, when the Madison County Board of Supervisors required that the county's bridges be covered, saying, "The expense of the roof is more than made up by the permanency of the bridge." Covering the bridges would protect them from rain, snow, and ice, extending their useful lifespan.

Madison County had two covered-bridge building waves. The first wave (1870 until about 1877) included the existing peaked-roof bridges. The second wave (approximately 1878 until 1889) produced all the existing arched-roof bridges, as David Hargrove and Walt Libby noted in "Covered Bridge News" in the January 30, 2019, issue of the *Winterset Madisonian*.

As modern farm equipment increased in width, height, and weight, the bridges posed a problem for farmers trying to move machinery along rural roads. Some covered bridges were destroyed in favor of an iron bridge that could accommodate the equipment and withstand Iowa's weather. Others were left in place, sitting forlornly next to the new iron bridges built to bypass them.

The county supervisors' logic for covering the bridges worked. "When these old bridges were taken down, the timbers were invariably found to be in a good state of preservation," noted Herman A. Mueller in his 1915 book *History of Madison County, Iowa and its People*.

While there were at least 18 covered bridges in Madison County in years past, only six remain. The covered bridges received a new lease on life following the publication of the 1992 novel *The Bridges of Madison County* and the 1995 film of the same name. Both tell the fictional story of Robert Kincaid, a photographer and free spirit documenting the covered bridges of Madison County, and Francesca Johnson, a local farm wife waiting for the fulfillment of a girlhood dream.

The Bridges of Madison County shows what it is to love and be loved so intensely that life is never the same again. As Robert told Francesca, "This kind of certainty comes but once in a lifetime."

KING BRIDGE SPANNED CEDAR CREEK. The King Bridge, also known as Badger Bridge, was in Lee Township in the northeast corner of Madison County. It was the smallest of all the county's covered bridges. Local farmer Jimmy King is shown here in the 1920s. This covered bridge was built by J.P. Clark in 1878. The county's decision to scrap King Bridge in 1934 and Brown Bridge in 1935 prompted calls to preserve the remaining covered bridges. (Courtesy Allen family.)

CEDAR BRIDGE ON THE MOVE. The Cedar Bridge was relocated in 1921 due to a highway expansion. It originally was built over Cedar Creek just north of Winterset. As automobiles and farm equipment grew larger, a stronger bridge was built at that location, so the old Cedar Bridge was moved to the next downstream crossing. The Twin City model 25-45 tractor pulling the bridge was a 25-horsepower heavyweight. (Courtesy Madison County Historical Society.)

COVERED BRIDGES AT A GLANCE. This 1957 postcard showcases some of Madison County's attractions that are still popular with visitors today, including the covered bridges and Clark Tower in Winterset City Park. The postcard shows seven historic covered bridges. All are still standing except the McBride Bridge northeast of Winterset, which burned in an arson fire in 1983. (Courtesy Allen family.)

BRIDGES MADE MADISON COUNTY A TOURISM DESTINATION. Covered bridges and tourism have long been synonymous with Madison County. Bus tours have been bringing visitors of all ages to the area for generations. This group of students and teachers/chaperones proudly displays a "We Like Winterset" banner around 1960. (Courtesy Allen family.)

IMES BRIDGE ON THE MOVE. The oldest of Madison County's remaining covered bridges, the Imes Bridge was built in 1870 and features a pitched roof. Crews moved the bridge in 1887, as was common back then, to a spot where it was needed over Clanton Creek southwest of St. Charles, near the Imes farms. The bridge was moved again in 1977 to its present location over a ravine just east of St. Charles. (Courtesy Steve Downs.)

IMES BRIDGE WELCOMES VISITORS TO ST. CHARLES. The Imes Bridge was originally known as the Wiggins Ford Bridge and spanned the Middle River west of Patterson on the main road to southeast Iowa. Since 1977, it has welcomed visitors as they enter Madison County from Interstate 35 at exit 52 near St. Charles, which calls itself "The Gateway to the Bridges." (Author's collection.)

Driving through Cedar Bridge. Cedar Bridge was constructed in 1883 over Cedar Creek north of Winterset on what is now US Highway 169. It was moved to its present location northeast of Winterset over the same creek in 1921. It is the last covered bridge that vehicles can drive through. Cedar Bridge is featured on the cover of the novel *The Bridges of Madison County*. In May 1993, Oprah Winfrey broadcast her daytime talk show from the small, landscaped park near Cedar Bridge. (Courtesy Linda Griffith Smith.)

Making Memories at Hogback Bridge. Built in 1884 by Harvey P. Jones and George K. Foster, the Hogback Covered Bridge is the last of the surviving bridges to be constructed. It rests at its original location in a valley northwest of Winterset, with a new bridge nearby carrying traffic. Hogback gets its unusual name from the limestone ridge that forms at the west end of the river valley. (Author's collection.)

The Famous Roseman Bridge. In the novel *The Bridges of Madison County* and the movie, Roseman is the bridge Robert Kincaid seeks when he stops at Francesca Johnson's home for directions. It is also where Francesca leaves her note inviting the *National Geographic* photographer to dinner. The Roseman Bridge still stands at the original location where it was built by Harvey P. Jones and George K. Foster in 1883. (Courtesy Madison County Historical Society.)

She Said Yes! Andrew Lauver of Lake City, Iowa, and Mary (Francque) Lauver of Illinois had their first date at the Holliwell Bridge in September 2017. The couple got engaged there on August 26, 2018. "We then drove around the John Deere dealership in Winterset, stopped at Casey's for a soda, and drove around the John Deere dealership again for good measure," said Mary, who married Andrew on August 24, 2019. (Courtesy Andrew and Mary Lauver.)

VISITORS MAKE THEIR MARK. Constructed in 1880, the Holliwell Bridge was named for George Halliwill, who owned the farm where it was built. The spelling of the bridge's name has changed through the years. Holliwell is the longest of the existing covered bridges at 122 feet, including the approaches. It is on what used to be the primary road to St. Charles. Visitors often sign their name and write other sentiments on the interior of the bridge. (Author's collection.)

STROLLING THROUGH THE PARK. Built in 1870 by Eli Cox, the Cutler-Donahoe Bridge is one of two remaining bridges featuring a pitched roof. Cox owned one of the earliest sawmills in Madison County. This bridge was originally over the North River near Bevington on land adjacent to the Donahoe family farm, which was later purchased by the Cutler family. In a move that covered 18 miles in two days, the bridge settled into its present site in Winterset's City Park in 1970. (Author's collection.)

Glimpse inside a Covered Bridge. Harvey P. Jones and George K. Foster, who built the Roseman Bridge, also built the Holliwell Bridge. Both are constructed with interior lattice work and an arched roof, as shown here on the Holliwell Bridge east of Winterset. (Author's collection.)

Commemorative Coins Showcase Bridges. Madison County has produced coins each year since 1970 to celebrate the Covered Bridge Festival. The 50th coin was sold in 2019. The one shown here from 1972 honors the McBride Bridge, which was built in 1871 by H.P. Jones and G.K. Foster and destroyed by arson in 1983. The man who burned it was distraught over a woman who left him. He later turned himself in. (Courtesy Madison County Historical Society.)

Book and Movie Made Madison County Famous. Anyone who has experienced the love of their life, a love that could never be, will understand why readers worldwide are moved by this novel by Robert James Waller. It became a best seller in 1992, and the popular 1995 movie was filmed in Winterset and surrounding areas. (Author's collection.)

Francesca's Kitchen. Many memorable scenes from the 1995 film *The Bridges of Madison County* were filmed in the kitchen of this 1800s-era farmhouse northeast of Winterset. The home was badly damaged when an arsonist targeted it in early October 2003, shortly before Madison County's annual Covered Bridge Festival. The two-story, wood-framed house was dubbed "Francesca's House," after lead character Francesca Johnson, portrayed by Meryl Streep. (Author's collection.)

REBUILDING CEDAR BRIDGE. Northeast of Winterset, Cedar Bridge has been destroyed by arson twice, once in 2004 and again in 2017. Both times, residents and organizations contributed funds to restore the bridge. This photograph shows craftsmen creating an authentic replica in 2005. A more fire-resistant replica was reopened to the public at the Covered Bridge Festival in October 2019. (Courtesy *Madisonian*.)

COVERED BRIDGE FESTIVAL. Winterset and Madison County have celebrated the Covered Bridge Festival each October since 1970. Organized by the Madison County Chamber of Commerce, the popular event includes a parade, craft booths selling local artists' creations, Passport to the Past activities at the Madison County Historical Society, tours of Madison County's six remaining covered bridges, and more. The 2020 Covered Bridge Festival was cancelled due to the COVID-19 pandemic. (Courtesy Allen family.)

Five

Winterset
The County Seat

Like many other county seat towns in Iowa, Winterset evolved from a suitable central location that could be traveled to and from any point in the county in a single day. There was more to Winterset's story, though.

A combination of factors, from productive agricultural land to an abundance of construction-grade limestone nearby, provided Winterset with a desirable setting. Even today, it is easy to see how the Madison County Courthouse and many 19th-century homes and businesses harken back to the early settlement of the town, beginning in 1849.

How did Winterset get its unusual name? Some early leaders suggested the name Independence, but others favored Summerset. Since cold, snowy weather had occurred that day, one witty pioneer said Winterset would be more appropriate.

In any case, Winterset swiftly emerged to a position of unchallenged dominance. Lawyers and other businessmen quickly set up offices in the new town and promoted the community's growth by establishing land offices, banks, and commercial businesses, including newspapers and stores. Charles D. Bevington became a leading business promoter, establishing a bank, investing in thousands of acres of land, and organizing promotional efforts for a railroad to connect Winterset with Des Moines.

By 1854, Winterset hit a growth spurt, leading to incorporation as a city in 1857. During this period, Caleb Clark and other stonecutters began to construct the limestone buildings for which Winterset and Madison County are known.

Winterset residents began to establish churches and schools as well. Six congregations had organized by 1858. This expanded to eight Christian denominations, both Protestant and Catholic, by the 1880s.

This was also the period when modern technology helped usher Winterset into a new era of prosperity. The coming of the Des Moines, Winterset & Southern Railroad (which soon became part of the Rock Island rail system) in 1872 prompted Winterset's second and greatest phase of growth and development. By 1881, Winterset had installed its first telephone switchboard.

From then on, Winterset has enjoyed steady growth. While the town had 1,500 residents just prior to the coming of the railroad, its population doubled to more than 3,000 by 1900. Today, this vibrant community has more than 5,300 people.

Devil's Backbone Mill. A ledge of limestone known as Devil's Backbone has defined the landscape southwest of Winterset for eons. Devil's Backbone offered a prime location for a mill in the mid-1800s. In the days before rail transportation, mills provided the pioneers with essentials like flour processed from locally grown grain. The area where this mill was located is now part of Pammel State Park, near the Harmon Tunnel. (Courtesy Allen family.)

Stagecoach Lines Connected Winterset. This advertisement from 1869 reflects how Winterset was an important hub for stagecoach travelers headed to Afton, Bedford, Clarinda, and beyond. The illustrated ad promotes the Winterset & De Soto Stage Line operated by Lothrop, Glazebrook & Tryon with four-horse coaches making east-west connections daily. (Courtesy Madison County Historical Society.)

Bevington Mansion on the Hill. Charles D. "Doc" Bevington built this elegant estate on the south edge of Winterset in 1856. The brick mansion has a limestone foundation and includes a number of interesting pieces, including a grand piano that was owned by the Bevington family. Windows with red glass imported from Europe, which are original to the home and indicate wealth, accent the front door. (Author's collection.)

Dr. Charles D. "Doc" Bevington, Pioneer. Ohio native Doc Bevington settled in Winterset in 1853 after heading to the California Gold Rush in 1849. He was one of the wealthiest men in central Iowa and owned more than 10,000 acres of Madison County land. He was married four times and had three children who survived to adulthood. Bevington died in 1903 and is buried in the Winterset Cemetery. (Courtesy Madison County Historical Society.)

SUSAN B. ANTHONY SPOKE IN WINTERSET. Susan B. Anthony (1820–1906) addressed the Winterset Women's Literary Society at the Madison County Courthouse on April 23, 1875. The well-known social reformer, abolitionist, and women's rights activist delivered a speech called "Women and Temperance" with many statistics and great zeal. "Her lecture had a good deal of Woman in it but little Temperance," charged the *Winterset Madisonian* newspaper. "Many of her ideas were wild . . . many of her premises were false." (Author's collection.)

DRIVING UP THE COURTHOUSE STEPS. While few specifics are known about this intriguing photograph, it is clear a man is driving up the Madison County Courthouse steps. The car has kerosene lamps, so it is likely this photograph was taken around 1917 or earlier. The Ford Motor Company often put on demonstrations like this to promote its automobiles. The soldiers in the photograph are likely members of the National Guard, which was active in Winterset from 1905 to 1917. (Courtesy Allen family.)

Afla Hutchison, Teacher and Corsetier. Afla Hutchison (back row, center) taught at the Doak School in Jefferson Township in northern Madison County in 1910 and 1912. Hutchison was also a trained corsetiere who helped women select the right Spirella brand corset. Her advertisement in the June 25, 1913, edition of the *Winterset Madisonian* noted, "My services are at your call. 710 East Washington Street, Phone 301-m." (Courtesy Madison County Historical Society.)

John Jones, Mail Messenger. John Jones, shown in an alley behind the west side of the square, died of pneumonia on New Year's Day 1907. His obituary in the January 3, 1907, edition of the *Winterset Madisonian* newspaper noted he carried the mail for years between the depot and post office and was able to "keep soul and body together on a salary of $10 per month." (Courtesy Madison County Historical Society.)

Greetings from Winterset. This postcard from the early 1900s shows daily life in Winterset, from people walking by shops near the Madison County Courthouse to streets humming with automobiles and horse-drawn carriages and wagons. All of these buildings are still standing in 2020, and Winterset remains a busy center of activity. (Courtesy Allen family.)

Sleigh Ride. Will Cummins and his wife, Ann, moved to Winterset in 1917. The Winterset water tower, which was constructed in 1910 on the same block as Monumental Park, is visible behind them. The shop in the photograph was operated by Carl Nielsen, a local photographer who worked in Winterset from 1899 until his death in 1940. Ann Cummins died in 1932 at age 80, while her husband died in 1933 at age 86. (Courtesy Allen family.)

DR. JESSIE SMITH. On May 26, 1907, Winterset physician Dr. Jessie Smith delivered a 13-pound baby boy who would grow up to become John Wayne. Jessie (Stauffer) Smith was born in Madison County in 1866 in a log cabin in Union Township. She married Mathias "Criss" Smith in 1889, the same year she enrolled in the Keokuk Medical College. Smith practiced medicine in Madison County from 1893 until she died from cancer in 1916. (Courtesy Madison County Historical Society.)

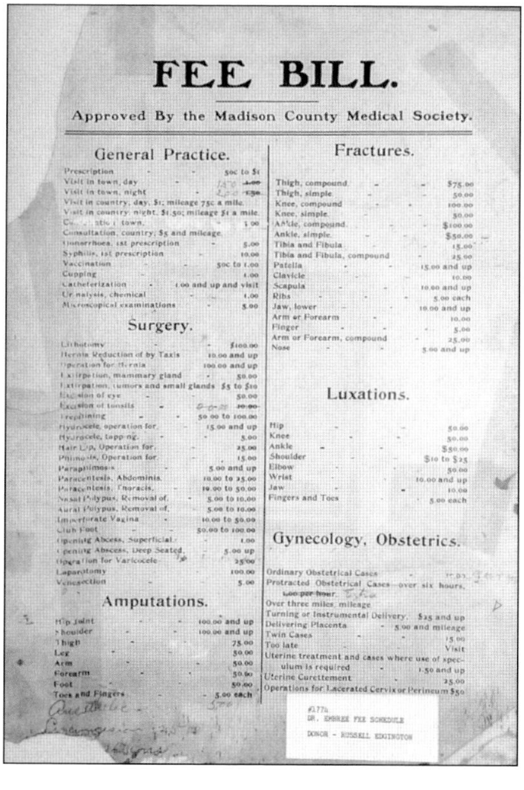

FEE BILL.

Approved By the Madison County Medical Society.

General Practice.

Prescription	50c to $1
Visit in town, day	1.00
Visit in town, night	1.50
Visit in country, day, $1; mileage 75c a mile.	
Visit in country, night, $1.50; mileage $1 a mile.	
[illegible] town	1.00
Consultation, country, $5 and mileage.	
Gonorrhoea, 1st prescription	5.00
Syphilis, 1st prescription	10.00
Vaccination	50c to 1.00
Cupping	1.00
Catheterization	1.00 and up and visit
Urinalysis, chemical	1.00
Microscopical examinations	5.00

Surgery.

Lithotomy	$100.00
Hernia Reduction of by Taxis	10.00 and up
Operation for Hernia	100.00 and up
Extirpation, mammary gland	50.00
Extirpation, tumors and small glands	$5 to $10
Excision of eye	50.00
Excision of tonsils	10.00
Trephining	50.00 to 100.00
Hydrocele, operation for.	15.00 and up
Hydrocele, tapping.	5.00
Hair Lip, Operation for.	25.00
Phimosis, Operation for.	15.00
Paraphimosis	5.00 and up
Paracentesis, Abdominis.	10.00 to 25.00
Paracentesis, Thoracis.	10.00 to 50.00
Nasal Polypus, Removal of.	5.00 to 10.00
Aural Polypus, Removal of.	5.00 to 10.00
Imperforate Vagina	10.00 to 50.00
Club Foot	50.00 to 100.00
Opening Abscess, Superficial	1.00
Opening Abscess, Deep Seated.	5.00 up
Operation for Varicocele	25.00
Laparotomy	100.00
Venesection	5.00

Amputations.

Hip Joint	100.00 and up
Shoulder	100.00 and up
Thigh	75.00
Leg	50.00
Arm	50.00
Forearm	50.00
Foot	50.00
Toes and Fingers	5.00 each

Fractures.

Thigh, compound	$75.00
Thigh, simple	50.00
Knee, compound	100.00
Knee, simple	50.00
Ankle, compound	$100.00
Ankle, simple	$50.00
Tibia and Fibula	15.00
Tibia and Fibula, compound	25.00
Patella	15.00 and up
Clavicle	10.00
Scapula	10.00 and up
Ribs	5.00 each
Jaw, lower	10.00 and up
Arm or Forearm	10.00
Finger	5.00
Arm or Forearm, compound	25.00
Nose	5.00 and up

Luxations.

Hip	50.00
Knee	50.00
Ankle	$50.00
Shoulder	$10 to $25
Elbow	50.00
Wrist	10.00 and up
Jaw	10.00
Fingers and Toes	5.00 each

Gynecology, Obstetrics.

Ordinary Obstetrical Cases	[illegible]
Protracted Obstetrical Cases—over six hours, 1.00 per hour.	
Over three miles, mileage	
Turning or Instrumental Delivery.	$25 and up
Delivering Placenta	5.00 and mileage
Twin Cases	15.00
Too late	Visit
Uterine treatment and cases where use of speculum is required	1.50 and up
Uterine Curettement	25.00
Operations for Lacerated Cervix or Perineum $50	

#177a
DR. EMBREE FEE SCHEDULE
DONOR - RUSSELL EDGINGTON

DOCTOR'S FEES IN THE EARLY 1900S. A visit with Dr. Edward Embree ranged from $25 to set a broken arm to $1 for a rural house call, plus mileage. An Indianola native, Embree earned his medical degree in Iowa City in 1889, began practicing medicine in Patterson, and moved to Winterset, where he built a large practice. Embree passed away at age 54 on November 13, 1918, following an extended illness. (Courtesy Madison County Historical Society.)

Hotel Provided Lodging, Jobs. This hotel was once next to today's George Washington Carver Park on Court Avenue. The hotel had various names through the years, including Shults' Hotel. It was later known as the Arcade Hotel. George Washington Carver was hired at Shults' Hotel as a cook after he arrived in Winterset in 1888. The horse-drawn omnibus in this photograph likely transported guests to the train depot. (Courtesy Allen family.)

Read All About It. Imagine setting all those lines of type to produce a newspaper. Winterset has had a number of newspapers through the years, including the *Winterset Reporter* (1895–1916), *Winterset News* (1873–1945), *Winterset Review* (1894–1901), and the *Winterset Madisonian,* which started in 1856 and is still printed weekly. The *Madisonian* office (shown here) has been in various buildings near courthouse square through the years. (Courtesy Madison County Historical Society.)

WATERMELON AT MONUMENTAL PARK. These men enjoying watermelon in Monumental Park include Tom Guiberson (left). They are relaxing in front of one of the earliest Civil War monuments installed in Iowa, a 14-foot marble obelisk dedicated on October 17, 1867. Monumental Park, one block east of the courthouse square on Court Avenue, includes Civil War–era cannons that were added in 1878. (Courtesy Allen family.)

PRESBYTERIAN CHURCH. Winterset's first Presbyterian church was established in October 1854. Eight charter members held worship services in the log courthouse in what is now Monumental Park. A permanent church was constructed in 1855. In February 1875, the congregation voted to build a bigger church with a 165-foot spire and capacity for 300 people. The church cost $14,000 (roughly $330,000 in 2020). It is still standing at 210 West Green Street. (Courtesy Madison County Historical Society.)

Fred Clarke, Pro Baseball Player. Fred Clarke was born on a farm near Winterset in 1872. A left fielder and left-handed batter, he signed with the Louisville Colonels in 1894 and was named manager in 1897. He joined the Pittsburgh (spelled Pittsburg at the time) Pirates in 1900 as a player and manager. He led the Pirates to a World Series championship in 1909 before retiring in 1915. Clarke was elected to the hall of fame in 1945 and passed away in 1960. (Courtesy Library of Congress.)

Jail to Retail. This building at 220 First Avenue North was constructed in 1901–1903 as a jail. Previously, the jail was in the Madison County Courthouse's basement. In 1895, a prisoner dug out of that "dungeon." The new jail served the area until it was decommissioned in 1993. Since then, the building has housed a variety of retail shops. (Author's collection.)

Haircuts, 15¢. While the names of these men have been lost to history, Winterset has had numerous barbers through the years. Many were mentioned in the April 13, 2011, edition of the *Winterset Madisonian*, including Nevin Landers and Denver Johnston, who worked together in the 1930s in a basement shop on the southwest corner of the square below Tom Kellogg's bar. Other Winterset barbers included Bud Farr, Gene Madsen, and Nolan Collins. (Courtesy Allen family.)

Bank President Built 15-Room Home. This lovely brick home that still stands two miles west of Winterset on the north side of Highway 92 was among the largest built in Madison County. Peter John "P.J." and Marcella (Monaghan) Cunningham built the 15-room home in 1918 with a solarium and many other amenities. P.J. was president of First National Bank in Winterset and later the Madison County Savings Bank. (Courtesy Allen family.)

Civilian Conservation Corps. The Civilian Conservation Corps (CCC) gave millions of young men employment during the Great Depression. In June 1933, men arrived in Winterset by train before heading to the CCC camp south of Winterset. They built Backbone Shelter at Pammel State Park in 1934 using oak logs from the site and limestone quarried nearby. While the CCC camp was dismantled in September 1939, the remains of the building foundations are still on the west side of Clark Tower Road south of Winterset. (Courtesy Madison County Historical Society.)

Creating Cedar Lake. A drinking water crisis began in Winterset when wells ran dry in the late 1930s, prompting the community to apply for a Public Works Administration grant in 1938 to build a reservoir. These funds were used to build Cedar Lake northeast of Winterset. Since 1939, Madison County residents have enjoyed fishing, picnicking, canoeing, and other outdoor recreation at Cedar Lake. (Courtesy Madison County Historical Society.)

FILL 'ER UP. There is a good reason why this top-of-the-line 1948 Chevrolet driven by Margaret Welch of Winterset pulled up at the Phillips 66 station. Welch's husband, Hugh, shown here washing the windshield, was the station's owner-operator from about 1945 to 1955. The station was on the northwest corner of John Wayne Drive and Washington Street. Glen Coffman is the man in the doorway. (Courtesy Allen family.)

CENTENNIAL PARADE, 1949. When Winterset celebrated its centennial in 1949, big crowds turned out for the parade, which is shown here marching east on Court Avenue. Note the vintage stop sign and the painted sign on the side of the brick building advertising Grace's Victory Café. (Courtesy Allen family.)

YOUNG MEN ENTER MILITARY SERVICE. These young men were outside the Club Café in 1951 on the east side of courthouse square, next to Grace's Victory Café/ bus stop, shortly before they left for the military. The group included Winterset High School graduates, from left to right, Bob Love, 19; Jack Benoit, 18; Paul Howell, 20; Phillip Hildebrand, 19; and Clifford Stephenson, 20; as well as Jim Koch, 20, of Adel. (Courtesy Allen family.)

TELEPHONE DIRECTORY, 1958. Long before cell phones were invented, landline, rotary-dial telephones could be found in homes and businesses around Madison County. This 1958 telephone directory provides a tremendous resource for historians, thanks to its business advertisements and histories of Madison County communities, including Winterset, Earlham, and Patterson. (Courtesy Madison County Historical Society.)

Dick Van Dyke in Winterset. Actor Dick Van Dyke (left) starred in the 1971 movie *Cold Turkey*, which was filmed in 1969 in Winterset, Greenfield, Des Moines, and Orient. *Cold Turkey* is a comedy about the fictional Iowa town of Eagle Rock, whose citizens take up a challenge to quit smoking for a month to win $25 million. Gary Allen of Winterset (right) enjoyed the fun. (Courtesy Allen collection.)

Cops at Montross Pharmacy. Montross Pharmacy and Gift Shop has served the Winterset community since 1922 and continues to operate a drugstore, gift shop, and soda fountain on the west side of courthouse square at 120 North First Avenue. In the 1960s, from left to right, Winterset police officers Dick Mapes, Gene Kirby, and Albert Lehman keep an eye on things outside the pharmacy. (Courtesy Allen family.)

Checkers at the Courthouse. Local men, including Glen Mercer (right), used to gather in a room below the south portico of the Madison County Courthouse to play checkers. Mercer worked in the auto salvage business in Winterset for years. Mercer, shown here in the 1950s holding his Iowa State Fair checker champion plaque, died in 1965 at age 62. (Courtesy Allen family.)

Homecoming Parade. The Winterset High School homecoming parade passed along the north side of courthouse square in this photograph taken in the fall of 1962. Mary Beeler, homecoming queen, waves at the crowd as she rides with her escort, Dennis Read, in a 1962 Ford Galaxie convertible. (Courtesy Allen family.)

GRACE'S VICTORY CAFÉ. Grace and Ralph Hendricks opened a café on the corner of First Street (now John Wayne Drive) and Court Avenue in 1945. Grace specialized in homemade cooking, including pan-fried chicken. After Ralph died in 1949, Grace continued to run the café until December 31, 1979. Grace had worked at the Wilson Hotel dining room in Winterset for two years and then at the North Side Café for 13 years before she and her husband opened their own café. (Courtesy Allen family.)

TRAILWAYS BUS STOP. Grace's Victory Café at the corner of First Street and Court Avenue served as a Continental Trailways bus depot starting in 1959. Prior to this, bus service was available through the Club Café in Winterset. The August 12, 1959, edition of the *Winterset Madisonian* noted that "Trailways is now running seven buses daily through Winterset. Three are eastbound, three are westbound, and one is southbound." (Courtesy Allen family.)

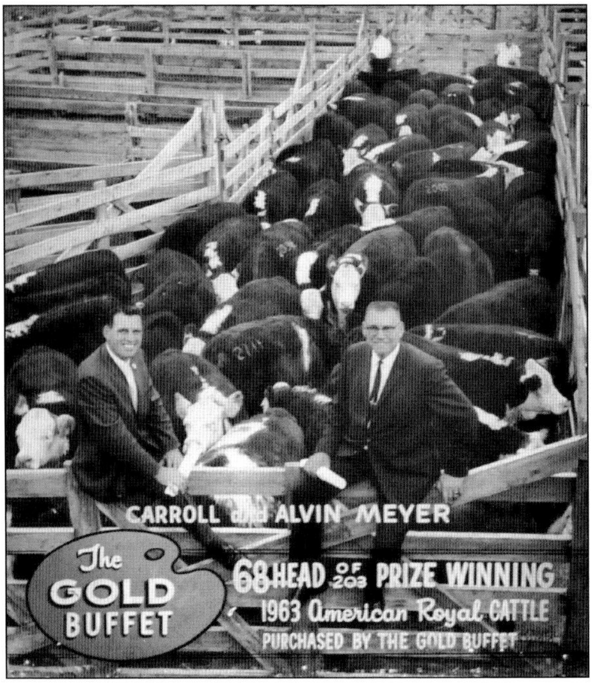

DINING AT THE GOLD BUFFET. The Gold Buffet drew people from miles around after it opened near the southeast corner of Highways 169 and 92 in Winterset in 1958. The 22,000-square-foot facility, known for its excellent food, also had a 10-lane bowling alley inside the building. "The Gold Buffet, an institution in the Winterset area for 32 years, closed its doors for the last time on Sunday," reported a front-page story in the *Winterset Madisonian* on December 27, 1990. (Courtesy Madison County Historical Society.)

BARGAINS AT RIDICULOUS DAY. Whether it was called Ridiculous Day or Crazy Day, the local chamber of commerce sponsored this event (shown here around 1960) for decades. When the *Winterset Madisonian* promoted the first Ridiculous Day, which was held October 28, 1955, it noted that "cooperating merchants are planning to offer a limited list of crazy specials. These will be selected items of merchandise at practically give-away prices." (Courtesy Allen family.)

NORTHSIDE CAFÉ. Harry Gaspari (above, right) operated the Northside Café in Winterset from 1920 to 1945. Gaspari grew up in Ireland and Scotland before moving to Des Moines as a young man. After relocating to Winterset in 1920, he purchased the Northside Café. He died at age 69 of a heart attack on the evening of August 28, 1956, while sitting on the courthouse lawn in Winterset. The historic Northside Café, at 61 East Jefferson Street on the north side of courthouse square, carries on a tradition of comfort food and hospitality. Chef Walter Jahncke (below, right) has been featured on the Iowa PBS show *Iowa Ingredient*. He is shown here in September 2020 with other staff members and a customer. (Above, courtesy Allen family; below, author's collection.)

Brittain Brothers in Standard Parts Store. Alvin "Bus" Brittain (left) visits with his brother Paul, who ran Brittain's Standard Parts in Winterset for years. A lifelong Madison County resident, Paul Brittain entered the salvage business with his father in 1929. In 1932, Paul went into the automotive parts business and was one of the first jobbers for the National Automotive Parts Association (NAPA). Bus owned Brittain's Furniture in Winterset for years. (Courtesy Allen family.)

Brothers Carry on Family Business. Brothers Chris (left) and Mark Brittain, shown here in September 2020, operate Brittain's Standard Parts at 113 East Green Street in Winterset. They are the third generation of their family to run this business, following in the footsteps of their father, Jerry, and grandfather Paul. (Author's collection.)

Frostee's, Always a Favorite. This little shop at 101 East Green Street is known for its homemade beef burgers (loose-meat sandwiches), breaded pork tenderloins, and cyclones (soft serve ice cream mixed with candy). The Dairy Sweet opened in this location in 1955. In the late 1980s, while Allison Acela Naber was still a Winterset High School student, she drove by the shop and hoped she would own it someday. She has owned Frostee's since 2007. (Author's collection.)

Winterset High School in Years Past. Placed in service in 1921, the three-story Winterset High School was touted as a "fireproof" building thanks to its poured concrete and brick structure. It served as a four-year high school through the class of 1969, when a new high school was built at the south edge of Winterset. In the following 40 years, the former high school served as a middle school, junior high, and school administration building. As of 2020, the building was empty, but options are being assessed to find new ways for it to serve the community. (Courtesy Madison County Historical Society.)

Pammel State Park. Four miles southwest of Winterset, the 350-acre Pammel State Park became one of Iowa's first state parks in 1930. Pammel is noted for its natural woodland beauty highlighted by its signature limestone ridge known as the "backbone." This includes Harmon Tunnel, which vehicles can drive through. (Author's collection.)

Fording the Middle River. Iowa became one of the first states to adopt a state park system, thanks to one of the nation's leading botanists, Dr. Louis Pammel of Iowa State College (now Iowa State University). In 1923, the state began purchasing land for Pammel State Park, which is named in honor of the scientist. Visitors can ford the Middle River, which flows through Pammel State Park. Fishing, picnicking, and camping remain favorite activities. (Author's collection.)

Madison County Freedom Rock. The Madison County Freedom Rock, painted by Iowa artist Ray "Bubba" Sorensen from Greenfield, is near the John Wayne Birthplace & Museum. The massive rock, which thanks veterans for their service and sacrifice, was dedicated on August 26, 2017. It honors local prisoners of war, the Winterset-based Quilts of Valor Foundation, and native sons John Wayne, George Stout (of "Monuments Men" fame), and Glenn Martin (pioneer aviator and entrepreneur). (Author's collection.)

Montross Pharmacy/Soda Fountain. The soda fountain and lunch counter have been part of Montross Pharmacy on the town square for generations. When George "Lloyd" Montross moved to Winterset from Sloan, Iowa, in 1922, he purchased the Niblo and Herring drugstore. This registered pharmacist managed the store alone until 1940, when his son George joined him. Other partners have included Earl Brown, Jerry Schwertfeger, Jim Nelson, and Jeff Olson. (Author's collection.)

BACK HOME

NATIVE RESIDENTS REALIZE THE GOOD LIFE IS RIGHT HERE IN WINTERSET

By Alan Cross

Spend five minutes talking with Winterset Mayor Jim Olson and you almost feel like packing up and moving next door to him.

"This is a wonderful place to live and raise a family," says Olson. "We have great stores for shopping, excellent medical facilities, incredible tourism and a fantastic school system.

"But the people who live and work here are Winterset's greatest asset."

Olson isn't a politician just looking to get re-elected when he brags on Winterset. He brags on Winterset because he has earned the right to.

Winterset is Olson's boyhood home, and he is one of the many people who grew up in Winterset and came back at the first opportunity to make it their home.

Iowa's 'celebrity' town

American icon and actor John Wayne's birth home is in Winterset, and three movies were filmed on its streets and surrounding countryside. The first was "Cold Turkey" made in 1971 starring Dick Van Dyke.

The last film to have used Winterset as a backdrop was the 2010 film "The Crazies."

It was, however, the 1995 film "Bridges of Madison County" which really put Winterset on the map, so to speak.

The Academy Award winning blockbuster film starred Clint Eastwood and Meryl Streep, and it was taken from the 1992 best-selling novel of the same name written by Iowa author Robert James Waller.

"The movie and the book have brought in a lot of tourism to Winterset," says Dave Trask.

Judy and Dave Trask own the Ben Franklin Store in Winterset. Both grew up in Winterset and came back to raise a family

www.iowalivingmagazines.com/winterset JUNE | 2012 Winterset Living

Dime Store Owners. Dave and Judy Trask (both 1964 graduates of Winterset High School) have run the Ben Franklin five-and-dime store at 72 East Court Avenue in Winterset across from the Madison County Courthouse since 1979. The couple received the Madison County Chamber of Commerce's Lifetime Achievement Award in 2014. Dave, a Vietnam veteran, served as the voice of the Huskies at Winterset High School football games for 25 years. (Courtesy Allen family.)

Courthouse Stands the Test of Time. Madison County, which was formed in 1846, first had a wooden courthouse, followed by a stone courthouse built in 1868. After a fire destroyed the stone courthouse in 1875, citizens rebuilt a second stone courthouse in 1876. This stunning courthouse, shown here from the west side of the town square in the summer of 2020, remains a hub of Winterset and Madison County. (Author's collection.)

Six

St. Charles

Gateway to the Bridges

Settlement in St. Charles occurred early in Madison County's history. In the 1840s, Missouri-born Joel Clanton and his large family settled one and a half miles west of present-day St. Charles. The town was established in 1852 about two miles from a Clanton Creek sawmill.

Among the prominent early settlers was Hogan Queen. He arrived in the St. Charles area in 1853, established a large stock farm, handled postal duties, and replenished stagecoach drivers at Queen's Point, his substantial stone house built in the 1860s. This gracious home is still standing and remains a point of pride for Madison County.

Located on the divide between the Middle and South Rivers, St. Charles emerged as a locally important trading point between Winterset and Indianola. This importance increased after the Des Moines & Kansas City Railway located a stop there about 1880. St. Charles became a local grain and livestock shipping center.

By the early 1890s, St. Charles boasted nearly 400 residents, along with a newspaper, four general stores, a bank, a mill, and other businesses. St. Charles's citizens also established schools and churches, including a high school that opened in 1886. Today, this heritage is reflected in a number of 19th-century buildings in St. Charles, which has approximately 621 residents.

The community remains attractive due to its close proximity to Interstate 35 and the Des Moines metro area. St. Charles hosts its annual Old Settlers celebration the third weekend in July. St. Charles is also home to the Avenue of the Saints Amphitheatre, which holds several music festivals each year, including the Hinterland Music Festival in August.

No matter what brings people to St. Charles, the historic Imes Covered Bridge welcomes everyone as they drive in from the east.

HERE COMES THE TRAIN. The railroad was once a lifeline for small towns like St. Charles. Passengers could travel to places near and far, while local merchants could access a wider variety of products from distant locations. Iowa had approximately 9,200 miles of railroad track by 1900, a number that peaked between 1911 and 1917 at more than 10,500 miles of track. (Courtesy Steve Downs.)

JOHNSTON BLOCK. John F. Johnston built this property on Main Street in 1900. Raised on a farm near St. Charles, he worked in the livestock-buying business before becoming a banker. When Pres. Franklin D. Roosevelt declared a nationwide bank holiday in March 1933, Johnston's bank was the only one in Madison County that remained solvent and continued business. While Johnston passed away in St. Charles in 1938, his building still stands. (Courtesy Allen family.)

St. Charles Cornet Band. By the early 1900s, many smalls towns like St. Charles boasted a brass band. These bands' repertoires relied heavily on popular songs, marches, and patriotic pieces. A small-town band was often called upon to play at all sorts of events, including fairs, Fourth of July celebrations, picnics, and political rallies. The band was a focus of community identity and pride. (Courtesy Steve Downs.)

Dray Service Made Deliveries. The words "Baggage Express" appear on the hand-painted sign on the side of this dray in St. Charles. A dray was a horse-driven wagon that transported goods a short distance, such as from the train depot to businesses in town. As technology evolved, trucks replaced drays, providing more power and speed. (Courtesy Allen family.)

WISE JEWELRY STORE. In years past, many small towns had a locally owned jewelry store. Wise & Son Jewelry in St. Charles offered watches, fine jewelry, and repair services. The shop (shown here in the early 1900s) was next to St. Charles's newspaper office. Note the dirt street and wooden sidewalk. Wise & Son was listed in the St. Charles section of the *Iowa State Gazetteer and Business Directory* in 1918–1919. (Courtesy Allen family.)

ST. CHARLES 1911 FIRE. In an era when many buildings in business districts were constructed of wood, fire was a constant threat. That was especially true in the winter, when heating stoves were in use. A large blaze in the winter of 1911 destroyed a number of buildings in St. Charles. The car in this photograph is a 1911 Ford Model T Speedster. (Courtesy Steve Downs.)

Rural Mail Carriers, 1908. Before radio, television, mobile phones, and e-mail, rural Iowa was often an isolated place. Trips into town to pick up or send mail were rarely made more than once a week. It was revolutionary when the federal government launched rural free delivery (RFD) in 1896. Farmers could get timely news via letters, postcards, newspapers, and magazines delivered by rural mail carriers like these in St. Charles. (Courtesy Allen family.)

St. Charles Opera House. When a small town had an opera house, it was a sure sign of progress. In 1905, the Methodist church (pictured) in St. Charles was sold to the city, and the congregation built a new church. The former church became the town's opera house, where Chautauqua events, including plays, were held. Silent movies were also shown here, complete with piano accompaniment. The opera house was just north of Main Street, behind the Johnston Block. (Courtesy Steve Downs.)

SCHOOL KIDS IN 1946. Providing local students with a high-quality education has long been a priority in the St. Charles community. This photograph of sixth and seventh grade students in St. Charles was taken in 1946. Today, St. Charles is part of Interstate 35 Community Schools, "which makes us loyal Roadrunners," according to the website stcharlesiowa.org. (Courtesy Steve Downs.)

JOHNSTON REST HOME. Older members of the St. Charles community could retire and spend their golden years at the Johnston Rest Home. Shown here are, from left to right, (first row) Jenny Herron, Eloise Aviatt, unidentified, Lulo Bolton, Linnie Shreves, and Lu Kale; (second row) Ola Johnston and Delores Gamble. (Courtesy Steve Downs.)

Methodist Church Serves Generations. The St. Charles Parish of the United Methodist Church is at 305 West Main Street. In 1858, a Methodist circuit rider named Murphy had a revival meeting in the home of William Porter. This started the first Methodist organization in St. Charles. In 1905, the Methodists sold their small, wooden church to the city and built a new church. A large congregation gathered there for this photograph, which likely dates from the late 1920s and was taken by Ogden Studio of St. Charles. (Courtesy Steve Downs.)

Funeral at the Methodist Church. William Frank Bradshaw died on December 16, 1958. His funeral was held December 19 at the Methodist church in St. Charles. Pallbearers included Clair Smith, Dean Smith, Bob Bradshaw, Billie Huglin, Dean Hampton, and Dick Brown. The total cost of the funeral was $592.50—more than $5,300 in 2020. (Courtesy Steve Downs.)

Working at the St. Charles Meat Locker. One is never too young to learn a trade. Leonard Beaman, 47; Dale E. Beaman Jr., 3; and Dale E. Beaman Sr., 25, are shown here at the St. Charles Locker in February 1958. Leonard and Lura Beaman opened the meat locker on May 17, 1946, and sold the business to the McClure family in March 1963. (Courtesy Steve Downs.)

Playing Cards at Home. Gathering friends and family to play cards is a time-honored tradition in small towns like St. Charles. Many communities had card clubs where members would meet regularly in each other's homes to play pinochle, bridge, or euchre. Folding card tables set up in the living room made it easy to entertain guests, as shown in this 1950s photograph. (Courtesy Steve Downs.)

Visiting at the Grocery Store. Brooks Grocery Store in downtown St. Charles served the community for decades. Owner Dean Brooks is shown here visiting with local police officer Bill Kuhns. Following Brooks's military service in World War II, he became the owner/operator of the grocery store, retiring in 1982. He passed away in 2003 at age 86. The building contains apartments today. (Courtesy Allen family.)

Church becomes Welcome Center. The St. Charles Welcome Center on Main Street hosts 8,000 to 10,000 visitors annually. At the east edge of town near the Imes Covered Bridge, the welcome center is in a former Presbyterian church built in 1916. The restored church includes beautiful stained-glass windows and a full kitchen in the modern basement, which also showcases photographs related to St. Charles history. (Author's collection.)

MONTROSS SODA FOUNTAIN. Montross Pharmacy, which started in Winterset in 1922, expanded to include stores in St. Charles and Earlham in 1978. All three pharmacies include a soda fountain. Nancy Cleland Ramey is shown at the soda fountain at the Montross Pharmacy on Main Street in St. Charles in July 2020. (Author's collection.)

GOV. KIM REYNOLDS. Iowa governor Kim Reynolds is a fifth-generation Iowan and St. Charles native. She credits her youth in St. Charles with teaching her the importance of community, love of country, discipline, and fiscal responsibility. During her career, Reynolds has served as Clarke County treasurer, a state senator, and Iowa's lieutenant governor. On May 24, 2017, Reynolds became the state's 43rd governor, and the first woman to hold the position. (Courtesy State of Iowa.)

Seven

Earlham

Small-Town Roots Run Deep

While Earlham is the second-largest town in Madison County, it was the first town in the county to get rail service when the Rock Island Railroad came into the area in 1869. Pioneer settler David Hockett donated land to the railroad and sold adjacent lots to new settlers.

Earlham had developed in northern Madison County when scores of Quakers (also called Friends) settled in the region during the 1850s. This area, known as the Quaker Divide, encompassed northern Madison County and the Bear Creek Settlement in southern Dallas County, Madison County's northern neighbor.

When it came time to name the new community in Madison County, a meeting was held in the home of Milton and Sarah Wilson. The group favored Sarah Wilson's suggestion of Earlham, derived from Earlham Hall in England and Earlham College in Richmond, Indiana, a Friends school in a community settled predominantly by Quakers. By 1892, the Friends at Earlham even established the short-lived Earlham Academy to encourage higher education.

After Earlham incorporated in 1870, the population jumped to more than 200. In 1871, the community built its first school, which is still standing and houses the Earlham Historical Society.

Earlham's growth was slow but steady, with a typical array of 19th-century small-town businesses, including a hotel, multiple general stores, a lumberyard, bank, and more. Limestone quarrying soon became the largest industry in the area. Quarries began opening in the 1880s in conjunction with the construction of the state capitol in Des Moines about 30 miles to the east.

Although local businessmen anticipated large sales to the builders of the state capitol, concrete makers purchased most of the lime by the turn of the 20th century. The Portland Cement Company, in fact, ran one of the largest operations. The Robertson Quarry, Nevitt Quarry, and Eureka Quarry all operated in the Earlham area.

Limestone mining remains a viable industry for Earlham, which includes 1,400 residents in 2020. Businesses in Earlham provide all the important conveniences of small-town living, including dining, banking, grocery shopping, health care, and an excellent school system.

Hockett House Museum. Earlham's history is preserved in this 1860s home of town founders David and Mary Jane Hockett. David Hockett (1830–1903) brought his wife and three children to the Earlham area from eastern Iowa by ox team and wagon in 1865. They settled on 200 acres where Earlham stands today. Hockett sold a third of his acreage for town development, making him instrumental in the founding of Earlham in 1870. (Author's collection.)

Earlham Makes Progress. Long before Interstate 80 was built across central Iowa, railroads offered the most efficient, modern way to travel. When the railroad reached northwest Madison County shortly after the Civil War, the new town of Earlham was laid out in 1869 and incorporated in 1870. This postcard shows how the town had grown by the early 1900s. Note the horse-drawn buggies and dirt streets. (Courtesy Earlham Historical Society.)

WELCOME TO EARLHAM POSTCARD. By the time this postcard was produced in the early 1900s, Earlham could boast a population of approximately 630 residents, along with fine new homes, a thriving business district, a busy railroad depot, the Earlham Academy for higher education, churches, and more. (Courtesy Earlham Historical Society.)

JUMP ON THE BAND WAGON. While many small towns around Madison County had their own brass bands, Earlham even had a bandwagon. The phrase "jump on the bandwagon" stems from this era. When the circus came to town, a bright, colorful wagon that carried the band drummed up excitement for the event. Politicians would sometimes rent a seat on the bandwagon so they could be seen parading through the streets. (Courtesy Earlham Historical Society.)

Earlham Academy. While Earlham built a public schoolhouse in 1871, local Quaker residents wanted to offer more educational opportunities. They were instrumental in establishing an advanced center of learning in 1892. While some of these visionaries had hoped to create a college, this dream never materialized due to insufficient funds. However, the private Earlham Academy was constructed for $12,000. (Courtesy Earlham Historical Society.)

School Assembly. This photograph was taken in 1916 inside the former Earlham Academy, which was at the corner of West Fourth Street and North Chestnut Avenue. After operating the private academy since 1892, the Quakers sold the school to the Earlham School District in 1900. The building was demolished in the winter of 1924–1925. (Courtesy Earlham Historical Society.)

Foster Captured Images of Earlham. Around 1900, Rollin M. Foster moved from Kansas City to Earlham, where he opened a photography studio. The Indiana native had a 40-year career as a photographer by the time he died in 1924 at age 66. His obituary noted that "Brother Foster was always a devout Christian man." Many of the distinctive photographs in the Earlham Historical Society's collection bear Foster's name. (Courtesy Earlham Historical Society.)

Joining the Bicycle Craze. Many of Rollin Foster's images offer compelling glimpses of daily life in Earlham's early years. While the name of this young man is not known, his joy is evident as he poses with his bicycle. The great bicycle craze that took America by storm starting in the 1890s launched countless Americans into a new kind of fun and mobility. (Courtesy Earlham Historical Society.)

Street Improvement Day. This group of local farmers north of Earlham took road drags into town in 1916 to demonstrate the need for better roads. Farmers in the photograph included Noell Neff, Earl Mitchell, and Jace Wilson, according to a handwritten note on the back. Dirt roads in the rural areas and in town turned to mud during inclement weather, making travel difficult, if not impossible. (Courtesy Earlham Historical Society.)

Earlham Harness Shop. In the days before the automobile was king, traditional horsepower was required to pull everything from wagons and carriages to farm equipment. This made Max Lilllard's harness shop an essential business for a farming community like Earlham. A pool hall would later be located here. (Courtesy Earlham Historical Society.)

Dry Goods Store. By the early 1900s, Earlham had a thriving business district filled with an array of shops, including a hardware store, grocery store, meat market, barbershop, drugstore, and more. This dry goods store displayed an amazing number of items in a fairly compact space, including many bolts of fabric. (Courtesy Earlham Historical Society.)

W.J. Barnett City Livery. When life moved at the pace of horse-drawn transportation, livery barns were big business in small towns like Earlham. Liveries served those who could not afford to own their own rig or needed to rent or store one temporarily, such as farmers who came to town and needed to protect their horses from inclement weather. Livery barns were a man's world, filled with the aroma of horse manure, harness oil, and hay. (Courtesy Earlham Historical Society.)

JOHN WAYNE HOME. Within a few years of the birth of their first child in Winterset in 1907, Clyde and Mary Morrison and their young son Marion (the future Hollywood actor John Wayne) lived in Earlham from 1910 to 1912. Clyde worked as a pharmacist in town. The home the family lived in during their time in Earlham (pictured) is a private residence today. (Author's collection.)

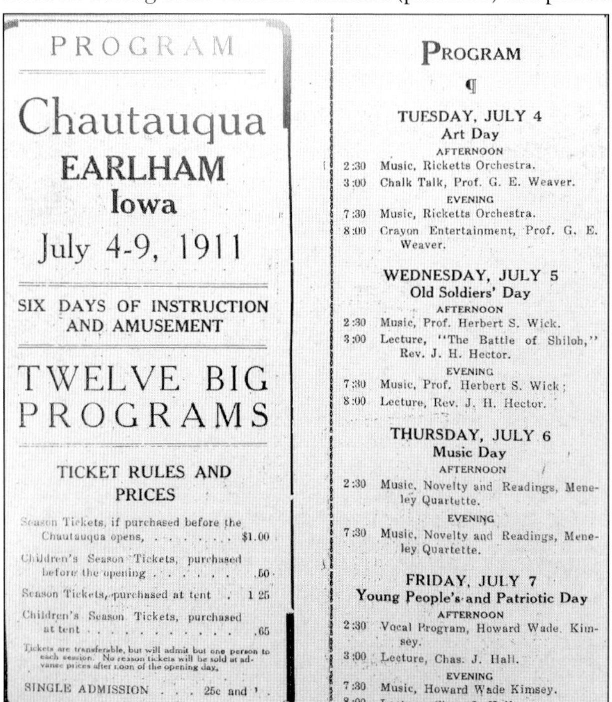

PROGRAM

Chautauqua
EARLHAM
Iowa
July 4-9, 1911

SIX DAYS OF INSTRUCTION AND AMUSEMENT

TWELVE BIG PROGRAMS

TICKET RULES AND PRICES

Season Tickets, if purchased before the Chautauqua opens, ... $1.00

Children's Season Tickets, purchased before the opening 50

Season Tickets, purchased at tent . 1 25

Children's Season Tickets, purchased at tent 65

Tickets are transferable, but will admit but one person to each session. No season tickets will be sold at advance prices after noon of the opening day.

SINGLE ADMISSION . . . 25c and

PROGRAM

¶

TUESDAY, JULY 4
Art Day
AFTERNOON
2:30 Music, Ricketts Orchestra.
3:00 Chalk Talk, Prof. G. E. Weaver.
EVENING
7:30 Music, Ricketts Orchestra.
8:00 Crayon Entertainment, Prof. G. E. Weaver.

WEDNESDAY, JULY 5
Old Soldiers' Day
AFTERNOON
2:30 Music, Prof. Herbert S. Wick.
3:00 Lecture, "The Battle of Shiloh," Rev. J. H. Hector.
EVENING
7:30 Music, Prof. Herbert S. Wick;
8:00 Lecture, Rev. J. H. Hector.

THURSDAY, JULY 6
Music Day
AFTERNOON
2:30 Music, Novelty and Readings, Meneley Quartette.
EVENING
7:30 Music, Novelty and Readings, Meneley Quartette.

FRIDAY, JULY 7
Young People's and Patriotic Day
AFTERNOON
2:30 Vocal Program, Howard Wade Kimsey.
3:00 Lecture, Chas. J. Hall.
EVENING
7:30 Music, Howard Wade Kimsey.
8:00 Lecture, Chas. J. Hall

CHAUTAUQUA IN 1911. Theodore Roosevelt called Chautauqua "the most American thing in America." From July 4 to July 9, 1911, people came to Earlham for "six days of instruction and amusement" with "twelve big programs" ranging from a lecture on the Civil War Battle of Shiloh to music by the Ricketts Orchestra. Season tickets could be acquired for $1. The Chautauqua circuit, which thrived from the late 1800s through the 1920s, brought culture and education to small-town America. (Courtesy Earlham Historical Society.)

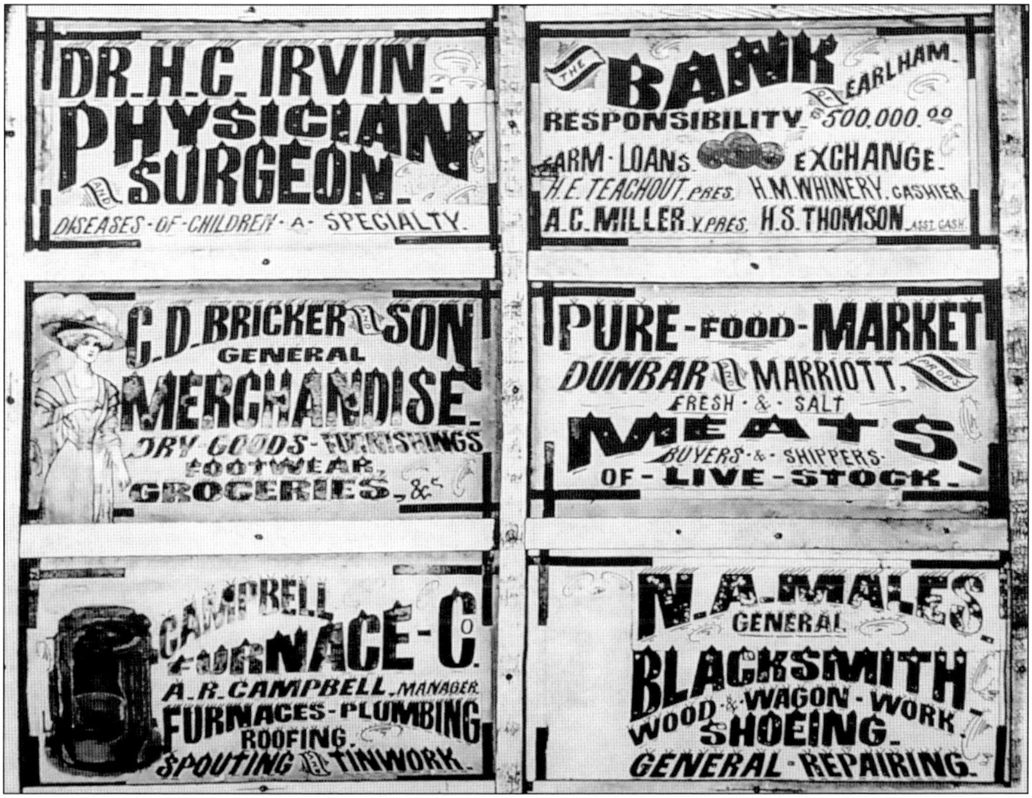

VINTAGE ADVERTISEMENTS. Various businesses needed to sustain a rural community like Earlham are represented in these hand-painted advertisements that measure 4.5 inches by 8.5 inches each. Twelve of these advertisements, from a blacksmith shop to a bank to a milliner, are on display at the Old School House Museum in Earlham. (Courtesy Earlham Historical Society.)

EARLHAM MASONIC LODGE. Freemasonry came early to Earlham, as locals worked to organize a Masonic lodge by 1875. The Masons reorganized in 1900, when the lodge was chartered as Madison Lodge No. 568. In 1921, the Masons and the Earlham Eastern Star Chapter 294 (a women's auxiliary) purchased the town's first public school as its new meeting place. This building currently houses the Earlham Historical Society. (Courtesy Earlham Historical Society.)

World War I Recruits. When the United States entered the Great War on April 6, 1917, thousands of Iowans stepped up to support the cause, both in the trenches and at home. According to the State Historical Society of Iowa, 114,217 Iowans enlisted in World War I. Those included these Earlham-area men shown in 1917. (Courtesy Earlham Historical Society.)

Earlham Arch. Earlham citizens built this arch in 1919 to celebrate the return of local servicemen from World War I. The 30-foot structure, complete with electric lights, was constructed in the center of Chestnut Street, north of the railroad crossing. The arch was later moved to the school grounds during a street paving project and repainted with "Earlham—A Friendly Town." The arch fell into disrepair and was dismantled in the 1960s. (Courtesy Earlham Historical Society.)

STUDENTS SERVED THOSE WHO SERVED. These Earlham fifth and sixth graders, along with their teacher Pearl Brauer, are shown in 1917 in front of the east entrance of the school. They were displaying comfort kits and knitted quilt squares made for World War I soldiers. Comfort kits (lightweight khaki bags) could include shaving supplies, writing utensils, letters, and other small items to make life a bit easier. (Courtesy Earlham Historical Society.)

OLD STONE SCHOOLHOUSE. The old stone schoolhouse was the first public school building constructed in Earlham (in 1871). It was built of native limestone from a quarry south of Earlham. A brick addition was constructed later. After the Earlham Academy closed in 1900, elementary school students attended classes in the old stone schoolhouse, while high school students attended classes in the former academy. (Courtesy Earlham Historical Society.)

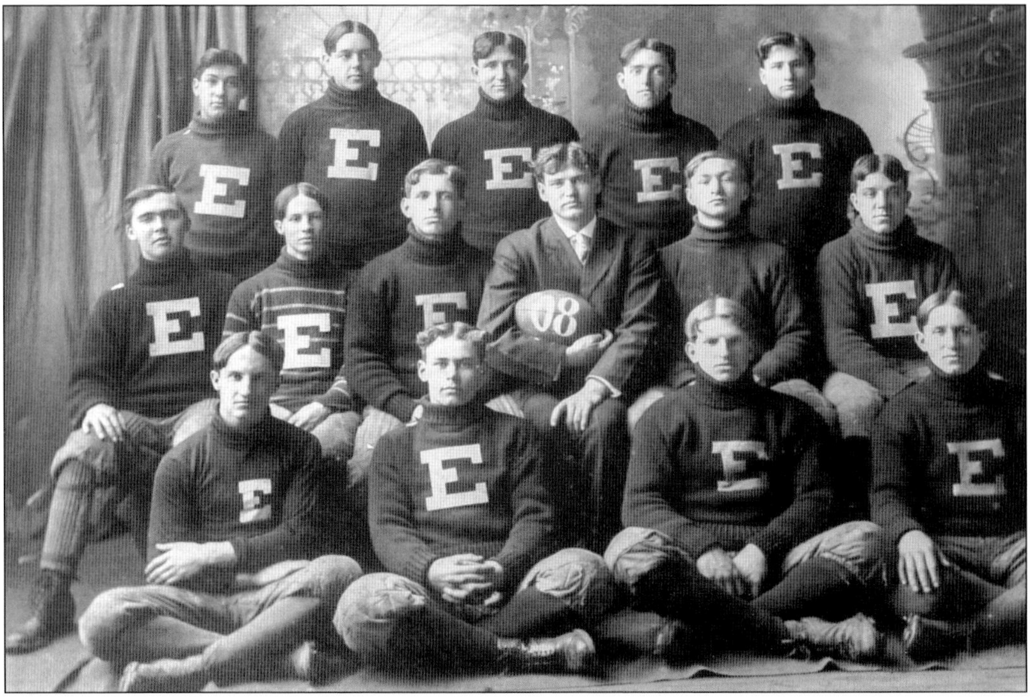

Earlham Football. High school football had become a popular sport in Earlham by 1908. Among the names listed on the back of this team photograph (which did not specify who was where) are Carl Bricker, Vergil Campbell, Cry Sulgrove, Arthur Francis, John Bechtel, Jim Irvin, Bert Fry, E.J. Nickerson, Harry Hunter, Ralph Thompson, Harry Irvin, Ralph Brooker, Fred Fry, and Willard Sulgrove. (Courtesy Earlham Historical Society.)

Earlham Girls' Basketball, 1916. Iowa was one of the few states in the early 1900s where girls' high school basketball was played. The sport thrived in small, rural schools like Earlham. The 1916 team included, from left to right, (first row) Mary Lentz, Hilda Ramsey, Princelle Thomas, Elma Clements, and Velma Dudley; (second row) Lucille Junkin, Coach Harold Graber, and Clara Rees; (third row) Esther Price, Lois Hoskins, and Irene Walker. (Courtesy Earlham Historical Society.)

Home Economics Class. These junior girls at Earlham High School, along with their teacher Helen Judy, were likely in a home economics class. By the early 1900s, educators began taking a scientific approach to make home life more efficient. Applying scientific principles to nutrition, sanitation, and other key areas gave women more time for pursuits other than cooking and cleaning. (Courtesy Earlham Historical Society.)

Earlham Track Team. Athletics, including track and cross-country teams, have long been part of Earlham High School. Note the silver trophy in front, along with the medals pinned to some of the boys' uniforms. It appears they won big that year. (Courtesy Earlham Historical Society.)

—ALWAYS A GOOD SHOW ALL-WAYS— Hang Me UP for Future Reference

EARL THEATRE

Two Complete Changes of Program Each Week: ❖ Earlham ❖ New Program Starts each Wednesday and Saturday

SAT., SUN., MON. MAR. 7, 8, 9
Mickey Rooney - Judy Garland
"BABES ON BROADWAY"
Mickey and Judy are at their best in this latest production
"Fair Today" — Cartoon

WED., THURS. MAR. 11, 12
James Cagney - Bettie Davis
"BRIDE CAME C. O. D."
Last Chapter "Sea Raiders"
Also added Short Subjects
BONUS NIGHTS

SAT., SUN., MON. MAR. 14, 15, 16
Abbott and Costello
"HOLD THAT GHOST"
Another One that will Roll you in the Aisles
Also Good Added Short Subjects
BONUS NIGHTS

WED., THURS. MAR. 18, 19
Elinor Powell - Ann Sothern
Robert Young
"LADY BE GOOD"
Starting New Serial Title
"RIDERS OF DEATH VALLEY"
BONUS NIGHTS

SAT., SUN., MON. MAR. 21, 22, 23
Errol Flynn - Fred McMurray
Technicolor
"DIVE BOMBER"
Also Good Band Act

Show Every Night Except Tuesday and Friday

EARLHAM LUMBER CO.
Lowe Bros. Paint
QUALITY LUMBER

UNITED FOOD MARKET
"QUALITY MEATS"
Earlham, Iowa

L.W.Caudle
INTRODUCING
Pennfield Paraland
Gasoline Fuel
Oils - Greases
Bulk Service
Ph. 44 - Earlham

SAT., SUN., MON. MAR. 28, 29, 30
Chas. Boyer - Paulette Goddard
Olivia De Haviland
"HOLD BACK THE DAWN"
Look at The Cast of stars and you be the judge of this picture
Also Good Added Short Subjects

WED., THURS. APRIL 1, 2
Don Ameche - Rosi'and Russell
"FEMININE TOUCH"
Another R. Russell Comedy Surprise
Chapter No. 3 Serial and Added
BONUS NIGHTS

SAT., SUN., MON. APRIL 4, 5, 6
Bob Hope - Paulette Goddard
Edward Arnold
"NOTHING BUT THE TRUTH"
Nuff sed—Remember "Caught In The Draft"
Also Good Short Subjects

WED., THURS. APRIL 8, 9
Jimmy Cagney - Pat O'Brien
"DEVIL DOGS OF THE AIR"
Also Serial—Added Short Subjects
BONUS NIGHTS

SAT., SUN., MON. APRIL 11, 12, 13
Jimmy Lydon - June Preisser
Martha O'Driscoll
"HENRY ALDRICH FOR PRESIDENT"
Also The Usual Good Added Short Subjects

WHAT'S SHOWING AT THE EARL? Earlham had a movie theater in the 1940s on what is now West First Street. The Earl Theatre showed movies five days a week. Admission was 45¢. In March and April 1941, patrons could watch stars like Mickey Rooney and Judy Garland in *Babes on Broadway*, James Cagney and Bette Davis in *Bride Came C.O.D.*, and comedians Abbott and Costello in *Hold That Ghost*. (Courtesy Earlham Historical Society.)

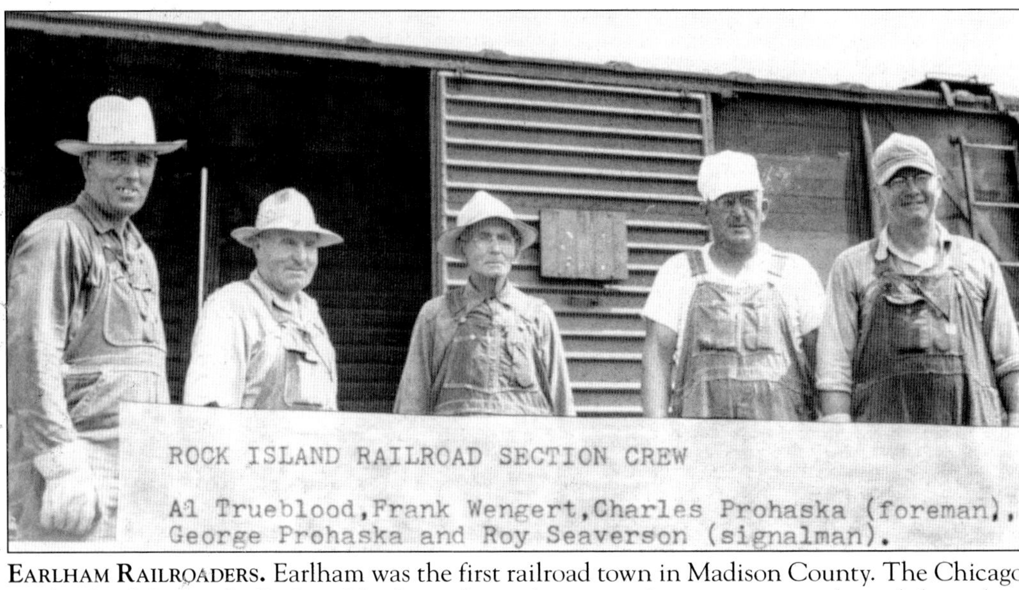

EARLHAM RAILROADERS. Earlham was the first railroad town in Madison County. The Chicago, Rock Island & Pacific Railroad built a side track, section house, water tank, and depot here around the time Earlham was founded in 1870. Years later, this Rock Island section crew posed for a photograph. From left to right are Al Trueblood, Frank Wengert, Charles Prohaska (foreman), George Prohaska, and Roy Seaverson (signalman). (Courtesy Earlham Historical Society.)

INMAN OIL COMPANY. As early as 1911, gasoline was sold from a barrel behind Elmer Scar's drugstore in Earlham. Filling stations developed as more people purchased automobiles. Powers "Pete" Inman built this filling station around 1941 and sold Conoco products through Inman Oil Company. His son Frank Inman later managed the company. (Courtesy Earlham Historical Society.)

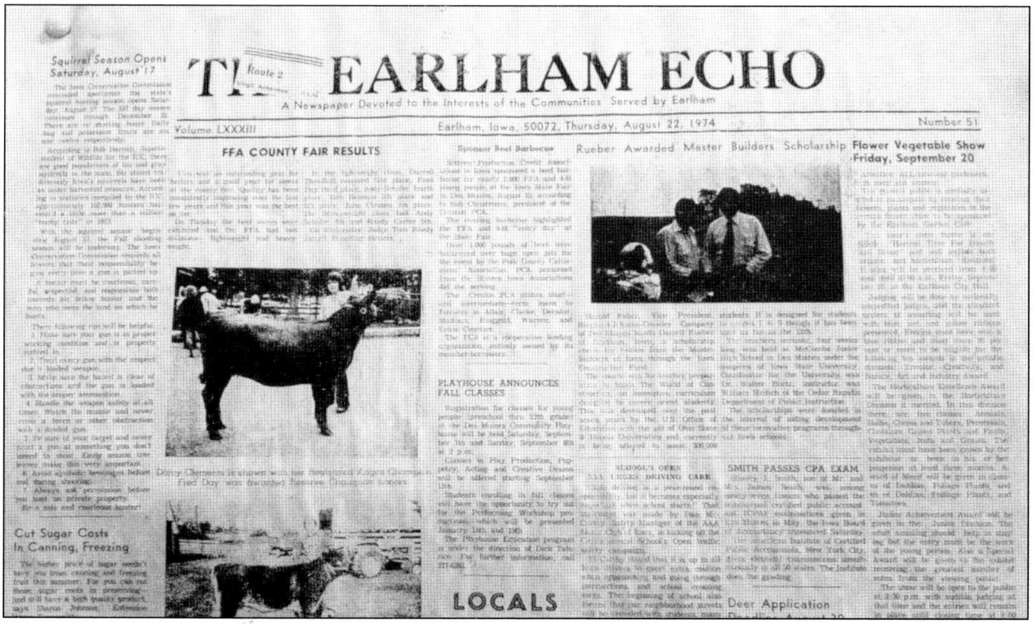

Squirrel Season Opens Saturday, August 17

THE EARLHAM ECHO

A Newspaper Devoted to the Interests of the Communities Served by Earlham

Volume LXXXIII — Earlham, Iowa, 50072, Thursday, August 22, 1974 — Number 51

FFA COUNTY FAIR RESULTS

Sponsor Beef Barbecue

Rueber Awarded Master Builders Scholarship

Flower Vegetable Show Friday, September 20

PLAYHOUSE ANNOUNCES FALL CLASSES

SMITH PASSES CPA EXAM

Cut Sugar Costs In Canning, Freezing

LOCALS

Deer Application

EARLHAM ECHO, 1974. The *Earlham Echo* was founded by a Mr. Livingston in 1890, when yearly subscriptions were \$1. Les Goeldner published the newspaper for 37 years (1934–1971). County fair results made front-page news in the August 22, 1974, edition shown here. The paper was published weekly until 1987. The *Echo* was relaunched in 2016, carrying on Earlham's weekly newspaper tradition. (Courtesy Earlham Historical Society.)

Native American Activist. Robert Knuth, who was born on the Sisseton Reservation (also known as the Lake Traverse Reservation) in South Dakota has spent part of his life in Earlham. He made the front page of the April 13, 2008, *Des Moines Register* in the story "Removing His Demons, Protecting His Heritage," which detailed Knuth's efforts to protect native burial grounds in adjacent Dallas County from a housing development. (Courtesy Earlham Historical Society.)

POW Larry Spencer. When enemy fire blasted Lt. Junior Grade Larry Spencer's F4B Phantom II during a reconnaissance escort mission on February 18, 1966, over North Vietnam, the Earlham native's captors ushered him into 2,551 days of beatings, isolation, starvation, and torture at the "Hanoi Hilton." "People ask, 'How do you endure seven years of that?' One day at a time," said Spencer when he spoke in 2005 at Camp Dodge in Johnston to honor Iowa's Vietnam veterans. (Author's collection.)

Bricker-Price Block. The Bricker-Price Block in downtown Earlham on Chestnut Avenue, seen above around 1970 and below in 2020, was built in 1900 by local contractor J.E. Walton. The C.D. Bricker general store was in the south half of the structure, while the W.P. Price building offered leased space in the north half. Second-floor offices were above both. The building, which is listed in the National Register of Historic Places, has housed a telephone exchange, apartments, and retail shops. A $2.1 million renovation began in 2017. The building now includes a restaurant on the first floor and event space with a kitchen on the second floor. It boasts 4,000 square feet with high ceilings and historic character. The project was led by Sharon Krause, whose husband, Kyle, is the CEO of the convenience store chain Kum & Go. (Above, courtesy Earlham Historical Society; below, author's collection.)

Hometown Market. A grocery store is a hub of any small town. Earlham has the Hometown Market (shown here in September 2020), which is on Chestnut Street downtown. It is close to other businesses, including the Montross Pharmacy and Bricker-Price Block. (Author's collection.)

Farm-to-Table Dinner. In October 2019, the Bricker-Price Block hosted its inaugural Harvest Gathering fundraiser. During this farm-to-table dinner, 80 guests were seated in the middle of Chestnut Avenue, with downtown Earlham's early 1900s architecture, including the Bricker-Price Block, as a backdrop. The four-course dinner paired perfectly with an evening of friends, family, community, and live acoustic music. Tickets for the 2020 event sold out in minutes. (Courtesy Harvest Photography.)

Eight

Small-Town Living
At Home in Madison County

During the early years of Madison County's settlement in the late 1840s and 1850s, many small towns sprang up across the county. Some of them, like Webster, Barney, and Pitzer, disappeared by the early 1900s as transportation routes changed and population bases shifted.

Others endured, even if they never grew to include more than a few hundred people. Bevington developed as a station on the Des Moines, Winterset & Southwestern Railroad, when a spur line was built in 1872 to Winterset. Charles D. Bevington, the town's namesake, spearheaded the arrival of the railroad to Madison County.

Bevington also sponsored the platting of Patterson, which got its start in 1872 with the arrival of the railroad. While the new community was supposed to be named in honor of railroad agent and merchant Alexander Pattison, a recording error resulted in the misspelled Patterson.

As with countless Iowa communities, the demise of one town and rapid development of another nearby demonstrated the railroad's tremendous significance in the 1800s. Consider old Peru. While it was settled in 1855, it perished in the wake of the 1889 development of a train depot one mile away at East Peru. Still, the region thrived, thanks to limestone quarries and agriculture, including a farmer named Jesse Hiatt who developed the famous Delicious apple.

In southwest Madison County in Grand River Township, Macksburg was incorporated in 1876, although settlers had begun to stake claims and farm in the area more than 20 years earlier. The town's namesake and first mayor, Dr. Joseph Mack, crusaded for Macksburg to become a railroad hub, an honor it did not receive. The town once boasted a general store, bank, and two churches. While it reached a peak population of 255 residents in 1940, Macksburg has about 118 residents today.

Just as the railroad was key to the 19th-century towns, a 20th-century development, Interstate 35 on the east side of Madison County, has influenced nearby towns, including Truro. Settlers began moving into this area in the early 1850s, and Truro was formed in 1881. The new town was originally called Ego, but this awkward name was dropped in favor of Truro, a growing community that currently includes 500 residents. Through all these changes, small-town living continues to be a major part of Madison County's charm.

WEBSTER CABIN/POST OFFICE. By the mid-1850s, forty small post offices were scattered around Madison County. Many disappeared by the early 1900s as transportation routes changed and population bases shifted. The town of Webster was laid out in 1855 southwest of Winterset. It had a post office (which is on display at the Madison County Historical Society) and a few other buildings before it faded away. (Author's collection.)

BEVINGTON UNDERTAKER. Otto and Julia (Miller) Bussanmas moved to Bevington in 1873 as newlyweds. One of Otto's businesses, Bussanmas & Son, was a furniture store with undertaking services. It had operated for nearly 20 years by the time Otto died in 1931. This ornate, horse-drawn hearse served the Bevington area years ago. By 1925, Bussanmas & Son, funeral directors and embalmers, advertised that it had "auto equipment." (Courtesy Maxine Bussanmas.)

Bevington Post Office. Located 12 miles east of Winterset near Interstate 35, Bevington was laid out in March 1872 and named in honor of C.D. "Doc" Bevington, who helped bring the railroad from Summerset in Warren County to Bevington and on to Winterset. The town once boasted the Bevington House hotel, a post office (shown here), general store, school, Methodist church, bank, and real estate office. (Courtesy Maxine Bussanmas.)

Patterson World War I Memorial. Local servicemen Jesse Russell Salsbury and Joseph Downs etched their names, along with the phrase "Shot in France," in the wet concrete base of a flagpole they erected on the day they enlisted in the military. Their haunting words came partially true when they were killed in a gas attack on May 27, 1918, in the French village of Cantigny, north of Paris. This was during the first sustained American offensive of World War I. The Madison County men were part of Company A of the famed Rainbow Division. A large crowd dedicated this monument in Patterson to the fallen soldiers on October 7, 1923. It incorporates the flagpole base with the inscription, now on its side. (Courtesy of Linda Griffith Smith.)

Dr. Mack's House Still Stands. Macksburg was named in honor of Dr. Joseph H. Mack, a pioneer settler from Ohio. This physician and Civil War veteran donated land for the town. His home in Macksburg was later occupied by his granddaughter Lela Wolfe and her husband, Glen, for a number of years. The stately house is south of the J.D. Craven Women's Relief Corps (WRC) Hall and Macksburg's town square. (Author's collection.)

WRC Hall Houses Macksburg's History. The J.D. Craven Women's Relief Corps No. 322 Auxiliary was organized in Macksburg in 1898. The WRC, the women's auxiliary of the Grand Army of the Republic, built this structure on the southeast corner of the town square in 1900–1901. The building, which is listed in the National Register of Historic Places, was sold in 2003 to local residents Ralph (pictured) and Georgena Breakenridge. The building is a community center and informal museum. (Author's collection.)

MACKSBURG BOYS' BASKETBALL. Voters in Grand River Township approved a plan in 1919 to consolidate the township's one-room school districts into one school system. The first senior class graduated from the new consolidated school in 1921. The new school also created opportunities for student athletes, such as these young men on the 1923 Macksburg boys' basketball team. In 1958, the Macksburg boys' basketball team competed at the state tournament. (Courtesy Ralph and Georgena Breakenridge.)

MACKSBURG CLASS OF 1956. After the Macksburg Consolidated School was created in 1919 and before the new school was constructed in 1920, students attended classes in the WRC Hall, the Independent Order of Odd Fellows Hall, the old school, and other locations in Macksburg. Today, the WRC houses many items of Macksburg High School memorabilia, including this 1956 senior class photograph. The last senior class graduated from Macksburg High in 1961 before the school became Orient-Macksburg. The Macksburg school burned in June 1997. (Courtesy Ralph and Georgena Breakenridge.)

Glenn Martin's Story Took Flight in Macksburg. Glenn L. Martin, an aviation entrepreneur, was born in Macksburg in 1886. As a young man, he was inspired by Wilbur and Orville Wright's successful flights in 1903. He later created the Glenn L. Martin Company, which designed the B-10 bomber. That company became the Martin-Marietta Corporation and Lockheed-Martin, a major US aerospace and defense contractor. Martin died in 1955. (Courtesy Kansas Historical Society.)

Welcome to Macksburg. While Macksburg's population peaked around 1940, when the southwest Madison County town had 255 residents, today it has a population of approximately 118. The town honors its history through this sign in the town park, which notes that the community was founded in 1876. "BulldogStrong" refers to the Orient-Macksburg school district mascot. (Author's collection.)

National Skillet Throw. The National Skillet Throw championships were born in 1975 in New Hampton, Missouri, where former Macksburg mayor Bill Sanders's brother was living. A number of Macksburg residents attended the event, which was moved to Macksburg for the town's centennial in 1976. The event drew 5,000 people, according to some reports. The skillet throw tradition continues to bring fun and publicity to Macksburg every summer at the town square, and generates community pride. (Courtesy *Winterset Madisonian* and Becky Faust.)

United Farmers Cooperative. A farmer-owned cooperative has long been part of Macksburg. While the co-op was part of the Afton-based Farmers Cooperative Company (FCC) for many years, FCC unified with United Farmers Mercantile Cooperative, based in Red Oak, in 2016. Since then, the Macksburg location (shown here in May 2020) has been part of United Farmers Cooperative, which provides grain facilities, livestock feed, agronomy products, and ag services for local farmers. (Author's collection.)

East Peru Postcard. East Peru thrived as the stone quarry industry expanded in the area in the late 1800s and early 1900s. The town's peak population of 371 occurred in 1910, according to the Iowa Data Center. Signs of progress are evident on this postcard from the early 1900s, which showcases the town's two churches, school, railroad depot, and equipment at the local limestone quarry. By 2010, East Peru's population had dropped to 125. (Courtesy Madison County Historical Society.)

Batter Up! Baseball was not just America's national pastime; it provided entertainment in rural Iowa for generations as well. Even tiny towns with a population of 200 to 300 people, like East Peru, could field a baseball team. This Peru baseball uniform is on display at the Madison County Historical Society in Winterset. (Author's collection.)

Delicious Apple Sign from Peru. While this sign is no longer standing, East Peru still displays another wooden sign in the heart of town noting that this area is the home of the Delicious apple. A descendant of farmer Jesse Hiatt's original Delicious apple tree, which produced fruit he called the Hawkeye apple, grows in a field a few miles northwest of East Peru. (Courtesy Allen family.)

Peru United Methodist Church. Countless weddings, baptisms, and funerals have been held through the years at the Peru United Methodist Church at 301 Brown Street. The church grew during a time when East Peru boasted roughly 200 residents. On a hill toward the edge of town, the church catches the eye thanks to its distinctive architecture. Completed in 1916, the church continues to serve its local congregation. (Author's collection.)

Truro Band. The first white settlers came to the Truro area around 1850, mainly from Ohio, and began farming. They also encouraged culture in their small community. Members of the Truro Band, all decked out in their uniforms, are shown here on the steps of the Madison County Courthouse in Winterset. (Courtesy Madison County Historical Society.)

Downtown Truro, 2020. With a population of 500 people, Truro in southeast Madison County may seem like it is in the middle of nowhere, yet it is connected to everywhere thanks to its prime location just west of Interstate 35. While the main business district is fairly quiet today, Truro once included multiple general stores, a hardware store, drugstore, blacksmith shop, bank, newspaper, two churches, and more. (Author's collection.)

Roadrunner Pride. Truro is home to Interstate 35 Community Schools, which serve students in Truro, St. Charles, East Peru, New Virginia, and surrounding areas. Interstate 35 High School in Truro is shown here in July 2020, complete with the school's Roadrunner mascot. (Author's collection.)

Podunk Center Store. Podunk Center made headlines worldwide when the store's owners decided to sell in 1969. The story was picked up by news wire services from New York City and Los Angeles. Homer and Gloria Weeks were swamped with offers from serious buyers who wanted to purchase the one-acre town. The couple originally set the price at $7,000, but offers reached $8,000. John Garr purchased the property. (Courtesy Allen family.)

"Hub of the World." While it might seem bold to call Podunk Center the "Hub of the World," Richard Greenwood, a former Winterset resident and Washington, DC, newspaperman, disagreed. "If you were a kid who lived there in the 1930s, it was the hub of the world, so don't laugh!" he said. In those days, about four families lived in the area, and farmers from a seven-mile radius exchanged eggs and cream for groceries and hardware items. (Courtesy Allen family.)

Podunk Center, 2020. In the rolling terrain south of Winterset and east of Macksburg in southern Madison County, Podunk Center was reportedly named by its first owner, Harold Morris, through a contest in 1934. In recent years, this tiny burg was known for good food at the local café. In 2020, the café was only open intermittently. (Author's collection.)

Nine

Famous Faces, Famous Places

Big Dreams Grow from Small Beginnings

For a relatively small, rural county, Madison County has produced a constellation of notables through the years.

Perhaps the most famous is Marion Robert Morrison, better known as John Wayne, who was born in Winterset in 1907. Since the John Wayne Birthplace Society was established in 1982, more than a million visitors have journeyed to the county to tour the birthplace museum and other sites connected with Wayne's history. Guests have included Pres. Ronald Reagan, movie legend Maureen O'Hara, and fans from 50 states and 40 countries.

The famous scientist George Washington Carver spent time in Winterset when he was a young man looking for a job and new opportunities in life. Thanks to the support and encouragement of local residents, Carver became the first African American to enroll at Iowa State College in Ames in 1891. After Carver completed his master's degree in 1896, Booker T. Washington invited him to join the faculty of Alabama's Tuskegee Institute.

Carver Park in Winterset was dedicated in 1988 to memorialize Carver's inspiring story. The pocket park is next to the site of the former hotel where Carver worked as a cook. A ceramic mural created by hundreds of Madison County students was installed in Carver Park in 2014. This public art project, the garden, and the limestone monument represent Carver's love of nature and art, his philosophy of service, and the story of how the people of Winterset encouraged him to reach his dreams.

Dreams also took flight for another famous Madison County resident, Glenn L. Martin, who was born in Macksburg in 1886. This aviation pioneer designed the Martin B-10 bombers that helped America win World War II.

And do not forget 1915 Winterset High School graduate George Stout, who made his mark on the world as his crew of "Monuments Men" saved priceless works of art from being looted and destroyed by the Nazis during World War II.

In recent years, Winterset became known nationwide as a quilting community, thanks to the popularity of *Fons & Porter's Love of Quilting* public television show, which starred Marianne Fons and Liz Porter. This influence, along with the opening of the Iowa Quilt Museum, helped Winterset become the national headquarters of the Quilts of Valor Foundation (QVF). The QVF is comprised of volunteers and members who create and present quilts to military members touched by war, no matter when or where they served.

George Washington Carver. Famed horticulturist George Washington Carver was born into slavery in Missouri around 1864 and came to Winterset in 1888. He attended the Baptist church, where he met Helen Milholland, the choir director who gave Carver singing lessons. She and her husband, Dr. John Milholland, encouraged Carver to attend Simpson College in Indianola. Carver went on to earn his master's degree at Iowa State in 1896 and join the faculty of Alabama's Tuskegee Institute. (Courtesy Library of Congress.)

Thankful Robbins. From the time she was born in 1845 in Indiana, Thankful Alma (James) Robbins lived the life of a pioneer defined by self-reliance. She married shortly after the Civil War and settled in Iowa in 1874. Her neighbors in Madison County often requested her assistance with medical issues. The self-taught Robbins was well versed in herbal medicine and inspired future scientist George Washington Carver. Robbins died in 1947 at the age of 101. (Courtesy Madison County Historical Society.)

John Wayne's Humble Beginnings. The story of Hollywood star John Wayne began in Winterset. He was born Marion Robert Morrison on May 26, 1907, the son of Clyde and Mary (Brown) Morrison. Since the John Wayne Birthplace Society was established in 1982, more than a million visitors have toured the birthplace and museum. (Courtesy Madison County Historical Society.)

Growing up in California. Back when he was still Marion Morrison, John Wayne is shown here while living in Keokuk, Iowa, with his father, Clyde, a pharmacist, and his younger brother, Robert E. Morrison, who was born in December 1912. In 1914, when Wayne was seven, his family moved to California. Wayne graduated from Glendale High School in 1925. By 1930, he had starred in his first major movie, *Big Trail.* (Courtesy John Wayne Birthplace.)

John Wayne Birthplace Museum. Opened in May 2015, this is the only museum in the world dedicated to John Wayne. Located at 205 South John Wayne Drive in Winterset, the 6,100-square-foot museum includes a movie theater with seats from Grauman's Chinese Theater in Hollywood. Visitors can explore the largest exhibit of John Wayne artifacts in existence, including original movie posters, film wardrobes, scripts, letters, artwork, Wayne's 1972 Pontiac station wagon, and more. (Author's collection.)

***The Sons of Katie Elder* Movie Exhibit.** Memorabilia from many of John Wayne's most popular films are displayed at the John Wayne Birthplace Museum. This exhibit showcases the 1965 film *The Sons of Katie Elder*, in which ranch owner Katie Elder's four sons determine to avenge the murder of their father and the swindling of their mother. The movie starred John Wayne and Dean Martin. (Author's collection.)

John Wayne Station Wagon. More interested in comfort and safety than show, John Wayne was often seen driving his automobiles around his home of Newport Beach, California. This 1972 Pontiac Grand Safari station wagon was customized by George Barris to accommodate Wayne's six-foot, four-inch frame. This distinctive car is on display at the John Wayne Birthplace Museum. (Author's collection.)

George Stout, Monuments Man. In the 2014 film *The Monuments Men*, a World War II platoon rescues priceless art masterpieces from Nazi thieves. Actor George Clooney's character, Frank Stokes, was based on George Stout, who was born in Winterset in 1897 and graduated from Winterset High School in 1915. Stout, a world-class expert in art preservation, helped reclaim thousands of pieces of artwork that Nazis had stolen across Europe. A monument honoring Stout was installed at the corner of South First Avenue and West Washington Street in 2018. (Courtesy Northside Café.)

Fons & Porter. Two friends from Winterset, Marianne Fons and Liz Porter, gained national fame when *Fons & Porter's Love of Quilting* began airing on public television in 2003. The pair developed a line of quilting tools and published many quilting books. Fons (left) and Porter (center) made an appearance in January 2020 at the Iowa Quilt Museum in downtown Winterset, where they met Linda Schminke (right) of Pella. (Courtesy Iowa Quilt Museum.)

Iowa Quilt Museum. The Iowa Quilt Museum opened in the former JC Penney department store (1931–1997) at 68 East Court Avenue in 2016. The museum welcomes quilt lovers, history buffs, and everyone who values American art and culture. The museum promotes appreciation of the art of quilting through quilt displays and information about quilt history. It is also the headquarters for the Quilts of Valor Foundation. (Courtesy Iowa Quilt Museum.)

Ten

Growing Opportunities

Reflecting the Past, Present, and Future

As it has from the start, Madison County continues to thrive from its rural roots, all while maintaining its small-town charm and mixing in plenty of progressive spirit.

Madison County excels at honoring the best of the past while welcoming new opportunities. Local businesses, residents, and tourists benefit from this ethos, which is clearly reflected in the county's historic courthouse square in Winterset.

The arrival of the railroad in 1872 fueled Winterset's greatest phase of growth and unleashed a frenzied period of construction. Many of the ornate brick buildings that grace courthouse square date from the 1870s and 1880s. While many Iowa communities experienced a similar burst of activity with the arrival of the railroad, Winterset has retained all its significant structures facing the square. Every building facing the courthouse has been in place since 1899.

Today, the Winterset Courthouse Historic District is listed in the National Register of Historic Places. Madison County as a whole continues to embrace its rich history while looking to the future.

Courthouse Square, East Side, North View. A lot has changed on this portion of John Wayne Drive since the photograph above was taken around the late 1970s. This view shows the Iowa Theater, the Coast to Coast hardware store, and the Western Auto store. The vehicles parked on the street include a Chevrolet Chevette, Chevrolet Caprice sedan, and Chevrolet pickup truck. The view below from early September 2020 shows the McGowen Hurst Clark Smith CPA firm at the corner of John Wayne Drive and Jefferson Street, along with the restored Iowa Theater, the Bakery Unlimited, Iowa State University Extension office, and more. (Above, courtesy Allen family; below, courtesy Jared McDonald.)

Courthouse Square, East Side, South View. In the 1950s (above), people could stop by the United Food Markets in the Masonic Temple building in the middle of the block, along with an appliance store, the Club Café, and Charles E. Tucker's real estate and farm loans business at the corner of Court Avenue. Below, in early September 2020, are Shawn's Furniture (in the former Masonic lodge), Salon 107, Mi Pueblito Mexican restaurant, and an antique store at the corner of John Wayne Drive and Court Avenue. (Above, courtesy Allen family; below, courtesy Jared McDonald.)

Courthouse Square, South Side, East View. In the 1950s image above, Court Avenue included Nichols Market, which offered groceries and meat; the Ben Franklin dime store; JC Penney's department store; and Harrison's dime/variety store. While the Ben Franklin dime store is still on Court Avenue, the block across from the Madison County Courthouse also includes the Iowa Quilt Museum (in the former JC Penney's), the Village Bootery, and more. (Above, courtesy Allen family; below, courtesy Jared McDonald.)

COURTHOUSE SQUARE, SOUTH SIDE, WEST VIEW. In the mid-1950s view above, the west end of Court Avenue included Woody Thompson Shoes, Harrison's dime/variety store, Graves Clothing, Breeding's Hardware, and Union State Bank. Shown below at sunrise in early September 2020, Court Avenue now includes Madison County Medical Associates, Madison County Mercantile, Bridges Financial, Piece Works Quilt Shop, and Anything Sweet and More Café. (Above, courtesy Allen family; below, courtesy Jared McDonald.)

Courthouse Square, West Side, South View. A variety of businesses that are long gone are seen above in the mid-1950s, including the Flatts store, Miller Drug, Grahams, and more. Below, the block west of the Madison County Courthouse is filled with shops in early September 2020, including the International Eyecare Center, Covered Bridge Realty, and a trio of upscale home furnishing and gift stores—Re:Home, Harvest Creek, and Pine Creek. (Above, courtesy Madison County Historical Society; below, courtesy Jared McDonald.)

COURTHOUSE SQUARE, WEST SIDE, NORTH VIEW. In the 1940s (above), North First Avenue west of the Madison County Courthouse included Rowe Clothing, Montross Pharmacy and Gift Shop, Easter's grocery and meats, King's Clothing, and more. Much has changed through the years along North First Avenue west of the courthouse. While Montross Pharmacy and Gift Shop has remained for generations, other shops seen below in early September 2020 include Angel Wings and Country Things clothing and gifts, Jeanne's Threads, and more. (Above, courtesy Allen family; below, courtesy Jared McDonald.)

COURTHOUSE SQUARE, NORTH SIDE, WEST VIEW. First National Bank anchored this block at the corner of Jefferson Street and North First Avenue in the image above. In the late 1920s and early 1930s, other shops down this block included the J.E. Hamilton land office, a harness and saddles shop, drugstore/jewelry store, and other businesses. The businesses in this block have changed tremendously in the past 100 years. In early September 2020 (below), businesses here include b shannon designs, law offices, Pro Team Insurance, Homefront Real Estate, the U.S. Cellular cell phone store, the historic Northside Café, and more. (Above, courtesy Allen family; below, courtesy Jared McDonald.)

Courthouse Square, North Side, East View. It was a busy day in Winterset, based on all the cars and trucks shown above in the late 1920s or early 1930s. People were shopping at the bakery and other businesses on this block. In early September 2020 (below), Jefferson Street north of the Madison County Courthouse includes Madison County Realty, Affinity Insurance Group, the China Café, and the Madison County Chamber of Commerce welcome center and gift shop. (Above, courtesy Allen family; below, courtesy Jared McDonald.)

Iowa Theater Renaissance. Built in approximately 1899, this iconic destination on the east side of Winterset's town square at 121 John Wayne Drive became a "first-class movie show" by 1914, according to the local press. The historic theater was restored in 2015 and now shows current Hollywood movies as well as classic films on Way Back Wednesday each week. (Author's collection.)

Pedaling through Madison County. The stunning views and rolling terrain of Madison County make the area a big draw for outdoor enthusiasts, including bicyclists. In July 2019, Winterset was an overnight stop for the Register's Annual Great Bicycle Ride Across Iowa (RAGBRAI), a seven-day extravaganza covering nearly 500 miles across Iowa. When the world's oldest, largest, and longest bicycle touring event reached Winterset, more than 10,000 registered riders rolled through town. (Courtesy *Winterset Madisonian* and Christa Braga.)

WINTERSET CIDERY. Five miles north of Winterset, the Winterset Cidery produces hard apple cider made with the juice from apples grown in the Midwest. Owners Nick and Niña Williams took over the cidery in August 2019. An array of craft cider flavors include apple pie, cherry vanilla, lime habanero, and Winterset, the flagship medium-dry cider that serves as the base for nearly all ciders produced at the mill. (Courtesy Linda Griffith Smith.)

PAMMEL PARK COFFEE. Matt and Naomi Hupton have been roasting small batches of exceptional coffees since 2018 at Pammel Park Coffee on their century farm southwest of Winterset, just down the road from Pammel State Park. Every batch is prepared with precision to showcase each coffee's unique attributes and flavor profile. Many of the company's coffee names honor Madison County attractions, such as the Roseman Bridge Blend. (Author's collection.)

CHAMPIONSHIP SOFTBALL TEAM, 2020. The Winterset High School Huskies softball team won the Class 4-A state championship on July 30, 2020, in an 11-inning game in Fort Dodge against returning state champion Carlisle. The Huskies upset the top-seeded Wildcats 4-3. (Courtesy *Winterset Madisonian* and Greg Harrison.)

COVERED BRIDGES SCENIC BYWAY. The Covered Bridges Scenic Byway, which was celebrated with a ribbon-cutting ceremony in 2018, offers visitors a journey into iconic America. Signs around Madison County guide travelers along this 82-plus-mile route, which includes the famous covered bridges as well as an array of natural areas, historical and cultural sites, and other unique destinations. (Author's collection.)

Bibliography

Andreas, A.T. *Illustrated Historical Atlas of the State of Iowa*. Chicago, IL: Andreas Atlas Co., 1875.

Davies, J.J. *History and Business Directory of Madison County, Iowa: A Complete History of the County*. Des Moines, IA: Mills & Co. Printers and Publishers, 1869.

Earlham Echo newspaper archives. earlham.advantage-preservation.com.

Earlham, Iowa: 1870 Centennial 1970. Self-published, 1970.

East Peru, Iowa: 1887 to 1987. Audubon, IA: Audubon Publishing Co., 1986.

Howell, Ronald. *The Rural Schools of Madison County: A Vanishing Heritage*. Clinton, IA: Clinton Printing Company, 2019.

Hulbert, Mae. *Old Settlers of St. Charles, Iowa, and a Look to the Future, Volume 1*. Self-published, 1991.

Macksburg & Neighbors. Self-published, 2002.

Madison County Chamber of Commerce. www.madisoncounty.com.

Madison County Historic Preservation Commission. madisoncountyhistory.net.

Mueller, Herman A. *History of Madison County, Iowa and its People*. Chicago, IL: S.J. Clarke Publishing Company, 1915.

Parrott, Pauline. *Grand River Township and Macksburg*. Self-published, 1997.

St. Patrick's Irish Settlement. Self-published, 1979.

The Union Historical Company. *History of Madison County, Iowa*. Des Moines, IA: Union Historical Company, 1879.

Truro Centennial, 1884 to 1984. Self-published, 1970.

Truro, Macksburg, and East Peru newspaper archives. winterset.advantage-preservation.com.

Winterset Madisonian, *Winterset News*, *Winterset Reporter*, and *Winterset Review* archives. winterset.advantage-preservation.com.